My First Trousers can be read either as a single book in its own right, or as the second in a series of four, titled *Soul Survivor Life*.

The aim of the series is to explain the basics of Christianity and Christian living in down-to-earth, jargon-free language. The four books follow the pattern of life: birth, adolescence, mid-life crisis and death. The first, *Walking with a Stranger*, explores what it really means to become a Christian, who God is and how we can build a personal relationship with him. *My First Trousers* looks at the challenges and rewards facing us when we start going deeper with Jesus. The Christian life is not easy, however, and *Weeping Before an Empty Tomb* asks how we cope when the going gets tough. The final book, *Afterlife*, is about facing the future, in particular death, heaven and eternity.

Mike Pilavachi is the founder of Soul Survivor and pastor of Soul Survivor, Watford. Craig Borlase is a freelance writer. They have previously written two other books together, *Live the Life* and *For the Audience of One* (both Hodder Christian Books).

My First Trousers

Growing up with God

Mike Pilavachi with Craig Borlase

Hodder & Stoughton

LONDON SYDNEY AUCKLAND

Copyright © Mike Pilavachi and Craig Borlase 1999

First published in Great Britain in 1999

The right of Mike Pilavachi and Craig Borlase to be identified as the
Authors of the Work has been asserted by them in accordance with
the Copyright, Designs and Patents Act 1988.

10 9 8 7 6 5 4 3 2 1

British Library Cataloguing in Publication Data
A record for this book is available from the British Library

ISBN 0 340 73535 X

Typeset by Avon Dataset Ltd, Bidford-on-Avon, Warks

Printed and bound in Great Britain by
Clays Ltd, St Ives plc

Hodder & Stoughton
A Division of Hodder Headline
338 Euston Road
London NW1 3BH

To Richard, Diana, Emma and David Scott.
You have taught me so much about what servant love
really means.

Contents

Acknowledgements

Thanks to all those who have paid the price for the writing of this book, particularly my friends and colleagues at Soul Survivor and the church family at Soul Survivor Watford. Special thanks go to Andrew Latimer and Andy Baldwin, two wonderful servants of God who have been such an encouragement to me, and to Chris and Belinda Russell, who came to the rescue in my hour of need. As in the past, I'd also like to express my appreciation to Matt and Beth Redman, who suffered with me in the writing of this book, as they seem to do with everything I'm involved in.

Introduction

I got my first trousers when I was ten. Maybe it was some kind of Greek-Cypriot custom that got brought over when my grandparents arrived before the Second World War, a hangover from the days when they lived in scorching heat nearly all year round. Perhaps it was because my parents wanted me to preserve my childhood innocence. Whatever the reason, it took a decade before my knees were covered with anything other than plasters or scabs, but when it happened, I was the happiest little chap in all of Harrow.

It wasn't as if I had spent my early years naked – I did have shorts to wear; anyway, as far as I could tell, trousers were just a bit of an inconvenience. When I was seven both my heroes wore shorts – Bobby Charlton and George Best – and that was good enough for me. Trousers were for boring sports like golf, darts and bowls. Real men got their knees out, and every other boy I knew did the same. But soon tragedy struck and my mates started to wear long trousers. Of course the first ones were ritually humiliated and considered to be 'a bit odd'. Us windy-kneed boys would stare menacingly at them as they walked into school. We made up stories of how they had wooden legs and avoided getting stuck with them at dinner.

Then the winter came and things got tough. At times it seemed like my boys were defecting on a daily basis, and the group of us that spent our lunch breaks huddled by the wall in the playground gradually became smaller and smaller. By the middle of the spring term, I was alone. All the other boys strolled happily around without needing shelter, while I, with blue knees and a worried look on my face, longed to have something more than just a pair of shorts around my legs.

I spent the next two years dreaming about trousers. I pictured myself collecting milk-bottle tops and sewing them together to make a pair of chinos. I asked my parents to get me out of shorts, but they told me that shorts were for boys.

'But I'm not a boy,' I squeaked.

Eventually I got them – I think it had something to do with me threatening to take them to court – and I was presented with the most magical present I have ever received. As I pulled on the brown, beige and chocolate coloured tartan trousers, my parents watched with pride in their eyes.

'You're a man now, Mike,' said my dad.

I felt like one too. I had finally graduated from boyhood, and it felt great. Strolling down the road to buy some penny chews I knew that I was on my way; people would respect me now, listen to me, even ask my advice about women, money or plumbing. In a couple of years I'd have a girlfriend and soon after that a Ford Capri with a loud exhaust. I was wearing my first trousers; I had made it and the world had better watch out.

A little later on I became a Christian. I was fifteen and thought I knew it all. Starting out back then was like being a child again; every day brought with it something fresh to get excited about, every day I was hungry to find out what would happen next. Instead of being in a playground or woods, my adventure was spiritual, and Jesus was my elder brother. It was just like being back in shorts again – racing around so fast that long trousers would simply get in the way. Just like when I was seven, and my knees were covered in scabs and bruises, the result of having too much energy and not enough wisdom. I made mistakes and fell over, but I was back on my feet straight away and ready to move on.

It makes me happy to think about those early weeks of being a Christian. These days we call it a honeymoon period, just like the time that newlyweds get to allow their love to sink in even deeper away from all the pressures of real life. I don't think I ever wondered if it would last, I guess I just assumed that it would. But of course it didn't. In the same way honeymooners return home and get on with their marriage, and just as children grow up to become the adult that is being formed within them, so I had to move on spiritually. It wasn't that I was forced, but just like when I had got tired of wearing shorts I wanted to move on and grow up.

God's into the idea of our first trousers. And our second, third and fourth. In fact, if each new pair of trousers represents taking a step closer in our relationship with him, I think it's fair to say that God would like us to have as many trousers as possible. God wants us to grow in our relationship with him, not because he hates kids or he prefers not to see our spiritual knees – he loves us at every stage of our Christian life – but he has so much in store for us that he can't wait for us to come and get it.

So this book is about getting your first trousers, moving on in your relationship with God. It's about the how and the why of getting to know God. It doesn't mean that God won't use you until you're snuggly fitted into your pair of 32 longs – God is most certainly into getting us started young – but as you move along in your relationship with him, you'll begin to find out even more about him. Talk to any godly man or woman and they won't tell you that they've made it or that they totally know God. They're much more likely to tell you that they've only just begun and that no matter how long they've known him, he still has fresh things to teach them.

Trousers crop up a lot in the Bible. OK, so you have to look pretty hard, but once you've found one pair, the rest just seem to jump right out at you. Here's a pair, from Paul's letter to the church at Philippi:

> I want to know Christ and the power of his resurrection and the fellowship of sharing in his sufferings, becoming like him in his death, and so, somehow, to attain to the resurrection from the dead.
>
> Not that I have already obtained all this, or have already been made perfect, but I press on to take hold of that for which Christ Jesus took hold of me. Brothers, I do not consider myself yet to have taken hold of it. But one thing I do: Forgetting what is behind and straining towards what is ahead, I press on towards the goal to win the prize for which God has called me heavenwards. (Philippians 3:10–14)

Now that is one seriously chunky pair of trousers. In kicking off with his thoughts about sharing the sufferings of the man who suffered more than any other man in history, Paul tells us that he is aiming high in his relationship with God. He's not after a Sunday stroll, taking it easy and not working up too much of a sweat. Paul's going for it big time, and judging by the rest of his letters, he means it too. It's something to aim for, don't you think? To be able to stand side by side with Jesus, sharing his pain as well as his power. As Christians – followers of Christ – our aims don't get much higher than that.

But Paul doesn't just leave us feeling bad with our jaws on the floor as we contemplate this superChristian who founded the Church. He goes on to explain how he's not there yet. He's still striving for it, still heading in the direction without having reached the final goal. He's not dwelling on the past, but steaming forward into the future, certain that God has good things in store for him and keen to find out what they are.

This is how we get our first trousers: by saying to God that we want to know more about Jesus, not just for the sake of knowing, but so that it will affect our lives. Moving on with God is about admitting that you're still learning, but instead of worrying about how little you know, concentrating on how much more there is for you to discover of God. It's about progress, that's all.

But, you might be thinking, what's the point of it all anyway, why should we bother moving on just because God wants it? There's one very good reason why we should bother: it's Jesus. Looking at the Bible it becomes clear that Jesus – fully God and fully human – made it his number one priority to keep in touch with his Father. I don't just mean that he spent time alone – although that was important – but that through his relationship with God, he showed what God is like.

If you want to get something out of this book, it would be a great idea to read it with your Bible next to you. There are plenty of stories taken from it and loads of verses quoted that you can look up for yourself. Everything that we believe as Christians is explained and described there, so it's worth getting into the habit of turning to it for inspiration and explanation.

As Christians we have been commanded to do a few things: love God, love our neighbours and get on with the job of telling the world. These are tough orders, but they apply to all of us who call ourselves Christians. It would be foolish to think we can follow them or even properly understand them without a continually deepening relationship with God. Over the years you'll go through plenty of different experiences, some of them good, some of them bad. If you aim to get to know God there are going to be loads of times throughout your Christian life that you feel as though you've taken a big step on in your relationship with him. Hopefully, what we look at here will act as a base on which you can build for many years to come. So what are you waiting for? It's time to try them on.

1

Everybody...Needs Somebody

THE MEANING OF LIFE

I sometimes think it's kind of strange that I – a swollen-bellied and gently maturing afro-haired bloke from Harrow – know the secret to life itself. Down the centuries men with bizarre names (the Platos, Socrates and Descartes of this world) have spent their lives pondering, musing and arguing about the answer to the eternal Why? I could have saved them the bother.

Before I get too excited, I ought to remind myself that I'm not alone – there are a few billion others who also know the score. You see, life is about just one thing – relationship. The reason why you and I, why all of us are here is to get as deep in with God as possible – soaking up all (and I mean *all*) that it means to be in touch with the Creator of heaven and earth.

Jesus came to earth because we weren't doing too well at getting on with our relationship with God. In some ways things are better now, but there are plenty of people who still have trouble hooking up with the Almighty. Still, so basic is our need for relationship that even if we don't get it from God – the very best source of relationship fulfilment around – we will always look elsewhere for compensation. Wherever you look you see evidence of this – most of the songs around are about relationships, so are the films, videos, magazines and TV shows. As for the soaps, well, where would they be without their constant feed of break-ups, let-downs, heart-aches and back-stabs?

But art imitates life, and all that we see around us is a reflection of what's going on inside each one of us. Relationships are as important to us human beings as oxygen and food. They're part of the 'Must Have' list that we cannot do without.

Back in the fifties someone wondered exactly what would happen if we did try to live without relationships. It seems outrageous now that they were allowed to do it, but a bunch of scientists actually managed to get permission to use twelve newborn babies as goalposts for their extended theoretical kick about. Six of the babies were given to their mothers as soon as they were born, the mothers being encouraged to spend as much time and attention on their new children as possible. Touch, talk, breastfeeding and eye contact were their staple diet. When the babies were asleep, they did so in a cot next to their mothers, so that they could hear them breathing.

Then there were the other six. These ones weren't quite so lucky, as no sooner had they popped their heads out and received a quick slap for their troubles but they were whisked away from their mothers and placed in incubators. Handling was kept to an absolute minimum, and breastfeeding was certainly off limits.

Throughout the month-long experiment, while their emotional supplies varied, each of the twelve babies were given exactly the same levels of nutrients. Once the experiment was complete, and the conclusions drawn up, the men in white coats made some startling discoveries. Those babies that were cared for so fully by their mothers had each put on an above average amount of weight for their age. Those who had spent their first thirty days in a sterile and inhuman environment all remained at their birth weight – having put on not a single pound. Yet they all had been pumped full of the same levels of baby-fertiliser. The fact that all the babies who had emotional contact grew so impressively makes it clear that loving relationships are good for us.

The results confirm what we all know instinctively: to grow and to be healthy we need relationships. It may start out as a mother's love, but it doesn't remain there. We need emotional nourishment like we need food – daily, right up to the point of death.

– And that's the truth today, we know that this is precisely what lies behind our craving for relationships. I doubt there's a single one of you who read about that experiment who didn't wince at the thought of keeping children away from their mothers for so long. We all recognise how unusual it is for human beings to be starved of relationships. We think it odd for a person to spend a lot of his or her life away from the company of other people, and that's why we are all fascinated by stories of people who have endured prolonged periods of solitude.

On 24 January 1972 hunters near the Talofofo River in Guam made an unusual discovery. Living in a tunnel-like underground cave they discovered Sergeant Shoichi Yokoi, a Japanese imperial army straggler who had lived entirely alone for twenty-eight years. This was not some stunt arranged by a Japanese TV game show, but a result of an attack by American soldiers in the dying months of World War II. Yokoi's unit was located in the Fena Mountain region of the upper reaches of the Talofofo River when the Americans landed on 21 July 1944. The Japanese troops made a night attack on the Americans in Nimitz Bay, but having managed to bring their tanks on shore, the Americans were on the offensive. At this juncture Yokoi's unit already faced a situation in which they would soon be forced to fight until the last man had been killed. Some of them managed to escape to the west shore of Nimitz Bay and ultimately to rejoin the main force in Agana. But Yokoi journeyed to the Talofofo area, and to the bamboo grove that would become his home for nearly three decades.

Yokoi, who had been a tailor's apprentice before being drafted in 1941, made clothing from the fibres of wild hibiscus plants and survived on a diet of coconuts, breadfruit, papayas, snails, eels and rats. 'We Japanese soldiers were told to prefer death to the disgrace of getting captured alive,' Yokoi said afterwards. 'The only thing that gave me the strength and will to survive was my faith in myself and that as a soldier of Japan, it was not a disgrace to continue on living.' No one in the history of humanity has equalled his record. Few have struggled with loneliness, fear, and self for as long as twenty-eight years.

Someone will make a film out of the story one day, but until then there are plenty of others out there that already feed our fascination for the tortures of solitude. Of all the films that have had an impact on me, two of the most significant have to be *Papillon* and *The Shawshank Redemption*, particularly the scenes where the lead characters are put through the horrors of solitary confinement.

Of course, this isn't just a theme that is confined to the movies. Down the centuries solitude has been cropping up in works of literature from all corners of the globe. From *The Count of Monte Cristo* to *Robinson Crusoe*, from western pulp fiction to ancient legend. So deep is our need for relationship that we are often fixated by tales of what happens when we go without. It's like standing inches away from a highly agitated poisonous snake at a zoo; the thrill comes from knowing that if we were inside the enclosure, there is a chance that we might not survive.

Sadly there are times when people don't just exploit our reliance on relationships for entertainment, but do so for personal destruction. During the two recent conflicts in the Balkans, allegations were made that high-ranking military officials used rape as a weapon against the Bosnians and Kosovan-Albanians. The belief is that soldiers were instructed to rape systematically large numbers of women in certain communities. This was not done merely to inflict a horrific evil on individual women, but to undermine the fabric of a whole society. Those who gave the orders did so because they believed that rape was the optimum way of bringing shame, mistrust, secrecy and illness upon entire communities for generations to come.

Christianity is about restored relationships. It is about being reunited with God, about him finding us and us finding him. Christianity is about God having created a people, a human race that would want to be like him, and that human race getting lost from him. He then took the steps necessary to win his creation back by becoming like the people he made. The epic story of the Bible traces God's relationship with his people and his search for them, his wooing of them and his winning of them back.

LOVING EACH OTHER

Christianity is also about our broken relationships being restored with one another as we come to know God. Many of us see that the problems of the human race are often caused by the breakdown of relationships: divorces, hatred, wars and violent crime are all caused by breakdowns in relationship. With all the progress that we have made as a human race, in science, in medicine, in engineering, in numerous other great feats, the one area that we have made no progress in whatsoever is in how to get on with one another.

Now I'm not going to come on all grand and wise here, but I do think that the twentieth century has been host to some fairly horrific things. Not only have we seen the development – and use – of the first weapon ever able to destroy life on a massive scale at the touch of a button, but we have also witnessed genocide more times than at any other point in history. Hitler, Stalin, Mao, Pol Pot, Amin, Hussein, Karadic, Milosevic – these are the names responsible for so much evil. But the hatred isn't limited to these few, as areas from Northern Ireland and Rwanda to

North American high schools and the hills of Kashmir have all seen the steady breakdown in human relationships. We don't know how to live together, and the reason we don't know how to live together is because we've lost contact with God who is the source of our life and who is the one who makes sense of our relationships with one another.

When God goes out of the equation, everything else becomes disjointed. As God finds us, peace comes. That's why the Bible speaks so much about peace and justice. That's why John says in his first letter, 'If we say we love God whom we have not seen, but hate our brother whom we have seen we are a liar.' Our relationship with God has to affect all our other relationships.

You may be reading this book because you've recently found yourself plugged into a relationship with God. As we've said already the theme of this book is growing up within that relationship, but it is important to remember that as our relationship with God deepens and grows, it affects all of the rest of our lives, and particularly our relationships with other people.

How do we grow in our relationships? How do we put things right? The first thing to realise is that many of us are carrying baggage: burdens from the past like bad memories of times when we were rejected, times of bereavement or pain. Whether it was a divorce or whether it was abuse, all sorts of different experiences we have faced still affect us now. Our relationship with God sets us free and brings healing to us so that we may again be able to relate to one another, not on the basis of pain, and not on the basis of brokenness, but as whole people.

Thankfully we have an example for this kind of lifestyle. Jesus was the one person who lived a life of wholeness in the middle of brokenness. He lived a life that was focused on God and others instead of being self-centred like the rest of us. For many of us, self-centredness is a result of pain – I know that for myself there's nothing more likely to get me thinking about my teeth than a decent dose of toothache, and so it is with our emotional states as well. Because we're in pain, we're self-centred. As God heals us of our pain, we become centred outside of ourselves; and that's how we were meant to function, because that's living in the image of God.

TRY THE BIBLE

We all know that any decent friendship between two people can only really exist if they spend time together, communicating and finding out how the other feels and thinks. Not surprisingly this is exactly how it is with us and God; our relationship with him can only really get off the ground once we get down to communication. I would imagine that for many of you communicating with a non-physical supreme life

17

force is not an everyday occurrence, which raises the obvious question of how? We can probably just about get our heads around the idea of prayer, but hearing God? For many that idea is not just weird, it's unnatural.

Hearing God is not weird and unnatural. Unusual – yes, but when it comes down to it, God constantly has something to say; the trick is knowing how to hear it. Want to know where to hear it? Try the Bible. We'll look later at how Jesus constantly quoted the Scripture – not to show off or confuse people, but because it contained the word of God. We need to get into the Bible for ourselves.

The trouble is that many of us are scared of the Bible – it's old, big and short on pictures. With a little work though, it really can come alive and make sense to any of us. There are plenty of excellent guides around that can help you read it every day; some of the best are *Every Day with Jesus*, a series by the United Christian Broadcasters (UCB) called *God's Word For Today* as well as *Disclosure* from Scripture Union. You should be able to find them all in your local Christian bookshop or in your church.

If you're going solo then the best place to start is probably the Gospels (if you're not familiar with the Bible, those are the first four books at the start of the second half of the Bible called the New Testament). These tell the story of Jesus and are guaranteed to amaze. You might like to keep on going once you've finished John and read Acts, the next book which explains what happened after Jesus went back to heaven. This history of the early Church is particularly helpful as it deals with many of the issues that we face today.

There are other ways of reading the Bible too. If you're a methodical kind of person you might want to read two chapters of the Old Testament and one of the New each day, perhaps chucking in a psalm and a few proverbs as well. Sometimes I love reading it as a novel: picking certain books and reading them straight through. The old history books of the Old Testament are good for this, particularly the ones called Kings, Chronicles and Samuel. At times you might like to read a passage as a meditation. You might only want to choose a small chunk or a psalm, but as you read through it slowly and think about it carefully ask God to show you things about it – try it with Psalm 23 first.

You could try studying the Bible – taking a passage and really working through it by finding out what other people have said about it. There are some great books around for this (called commentaries), and you'll have the added bonus of sounding like you've done years of research at the end of it. You might also want to try memorising verses. Find one you like and write it down somewhere that you will look at often. Learning bits of the Bible helps it become part of our lives, just as it ought to. Whatever you decide

19

to do – and I hope you might try all of these in time – don't just think of the Bible as something to be read for entertainment; use it to help you get closer to God.

LIVING THE TRUTH

Jesus knows exactly what we're like – and that includes our weaknesses as well as our strengths. Even though we can read the Bible and find out what he might be saying to us, we need to be able to do more than just mouth the words, but believe them with all our heart. Jesus knew this was the score and at one point said to people, 'Why do you call me "Lord, Lord," and do not do what I say?' He then talked about the man who not only heard the words of Jesus but also put them into practice (see Luke 6:46–9). Jesus said he was like the man who, when building a house, dug down deep and laid the foundations on a rock while his friend only laid foundations on sand. It was not that one built in the desert and the other by a mountain: both were beach houses. The difference lay in how deep the foundations were. The wise man kept digging through the sand until he found rock. When the rain and wind hit the beach his place stood firm while Mr Blag-It found himself sleeping out under the stars. When the storms come to us how deep are our foundations? Are they prepared to withstand the onslaught? So how do we dig deep? By not only hearing the words of our God but also putting them into practice.

Some of us are experience junkies; we leap from one emotionally charged experience to another as if Christianity was just a spiritual rollercoaster and we had a season ticket. Others are teaching junkies and that can be almost as bad. We desperately want to have listened to *that* tape, gone to *the* seminar or read *this* book. For some of us the need is not for more experiences or more teaching, the need is to begin to live out what we already know. Simply to have input (teaching) with no output (obedience to that teaching) will not result in growing Christians, just fat ones. Believe me – I'm a living advert for the results of a life without much exercise.

John Wimber – an American church leader who died in 1998 – had a classic answer for those in his church who complained that they wanted more meaty teaching. 'The meat's on the streets!' he would say. Jesus said, 'My food is to do the will of him who sent me.' The meat is on the streets. We must find our nourishment from living out the truth of the gospel and not just reading about it.

I am often tempted to call the things that keep me apart from God 'my little weakness' or 'what I do when I'm tired'. These phrases sound quite cute, don't they? The trouble comes when we believe them. It's vital that we Christians perform regular safety checks on ourselves, and I'm convinced that one of the best ones is to have friends in the church to whom we make ourselves accountable. This is something we must choose to do, and it doesn't work if it is forced upon us. There is a guy I hardly know who comes up to me at Christian conferences and asks me how my prayer life is and whether I would like to confess any lustful thoughts to him. So far I have resisted the temptation to punch him. The thing is, he is a stranger. My friends on the other hand know I want them to tell me anything they notice about my attitudes or behaviour which worries them. I know that part of my safety lies in being accountable to them. By having these relationships I am able to be honest instead of cute, calling it by its real name: sin.

I so want to finish the race set before me and not trip myself up on the last lap. So, I resolve to pursue a relationship with Jesus with all that is in me, to read his word and try to live it out, and to stay honest with him and the brothers and sisters he has given me.

God likes that. In the coming chapters we will look at Jesus, whose perfect life illustrates how we can grow into living a life that is marked by an intimate relationship with the Father. Because of that intimacy, we will naturally want to do what God tells us, and by being open to him and the Holy Spirit, by hearing the things that he wants us to do, we will end up getting out and taking God's goodness to the people who don't know him. With that compassion as our lifeblood, we will kick-start relationships with other people which express the very heart of God. And that, my friend, is what it means to grow as a Christian.

2

Getting Intimate

DEVELOPING THE RELATIONSHIP

That classic piece of British cinema *Nuns on the Run* tells the story of two petty criminals who – having stolen a million pounds from their gangland boss – take refuge in a convent, posing as visiting nuns. The crooks happen to be about as convincing as Christians as they are as women and throughout the ninety minutes the laughs keep coming as we see the would-be nuns having a fag, swearing, trying to take confession and getting excited when they end up in the female changing rooms after sport. The highlight for me comes when Sister Amnesia – played by Robbie Coltrane – tries to explain the Trinity (the basic Christian understanding that the Father, Jesus and the Holy Spirit are both one God and three persons – all at the same time!).

'Well,' he/she says to a confused baby Christian,

'it's like a shamrock: three leaves and one plant.' He then delivers a cheerful rhyme that goes 'two in three and three in two; flush them all down the loo.' Hardly Oscar material, I admit, but it made me laugh at the time.

The fact that Sister Amnesia struggled to explain the Trinity will probably come as no surprise to you. After all, how many of us can explain how God can be separate from himself at the same time as being part of himself at the same time as being the Holy Spirit all at the same time as being Jesus? Tricky one, yes? Theologians and people with beards have argued over this point for centuries, and I don't think that I'm in much of a position to be able to help. Perhaps this is one of the eternal mysteries that will only be fully revealed when we meet up with the three of them later. In the meantime though, what you and I can do is try to understand how best to develop a decently full relationship with the Father and the rest of that strange spiritual shamrock.

So where do we look? To Jesus. God made the point of sending him down to earth both as 100 per cent God and 100 per cent human – yeah, I know it's confusing – and consequently we have a fantastically full picture of the best way for us humans to relate to God. After all, if his own perfect and loving Son can't have a good relationship with him then who can? But thinking about father/son relationships as you know them might lead you down the wrong path; there were no tantrums, groundings or teething troubles between these two, just a vibrant, intense and totally mature relationship that was characterised by one special thing: intimacy. Remember how we spent the last chapter banging on about how important it is to have relationships? Well this is phase two: how to get the best, from God.

Jesus's relationship with his Father had intimacy written all over it. From the moment of his birth all the way through to the moment of his death and beyond the two were able to communicate and express love in a way that no other human relationship has ever come close to. The Gospels provide enough information to build up a picture of Jesus that shows exactly how important his intimate relationship with his Father was. Not only did it provide him with support, inspiration and affirmation, but it shows us that through Jesus's death, we too can get close to the Father and enjoy the same degree of intimacy with him.

Looking through the first four books of the New Testament that go to make up the story of Jesus's life, we see a number of times when that life went through major events. Just before he was about to start his final phase, travelling, preaching and healing, Jesus spent a big old chunk of time on his own in the desert. For forty days and nights he ate and drank nothing and resisted the temptations of the devil.

This is the first record that we have of him spending time alone, and while the reports of it focus mainly on the temptations of the devil, we do know that he responded to each attack by quoting Scripture. While any conclusion about direct communication between the two of them might have to be left in the air, we know for sure that Jesus concentrated his mind on the truth about God as it was expressed through the Bible.

These passages gave him strength. When Satan first tempted him by offering a solution to his extreme physical hunger, he was playing on the idea that Jesus may have needed to prove himself by firing off a quick miracle. He was also getting to work on any doubts that God would deliver the goods as a provider, but neither sides of the attack worked; Jesus quoted Deuteronomy 8:3, telling Satan that he was 100 per cent dependent on God.

The next temptation probed Jesus for any sense of insecurity about whether God would be able to protect him. Perhaps Satan wondered whether Jesus would give in to a sense of pride that he could test God and win, but, whatever the idea, Jesus again brushed him aside by reminding him that God was not to be tested and that his plan was to be trusted, quoting Deuteronomy 6:16.

Finally Satan probed the Son of God for any psychological need for significance, power or achievement. Jesus told him straight that there would be no compromising when it came to evil, quoting Deuteronomy 6:13. He brought the focus back onto God and the devil was sent packing.

Immediately after this period alone Jesus went straight out and began to preach. He had been fired up by the experience and was sure of who he was and what he was there for. Spending time with God – through his word as well as in prayer – had helped him take a giant step towards fulfilling his destiny.

Going to the other end of his life we see a clear example of how Jesus spent time with his Father. Having finished the last supper, Jesus knew that his arrest and trial were only hours away. He chose to spend his last night of freedom praying in the garden of Gethsemane. Jesus flung himself face down on the ground and cried, 'My Father, if it is possible, may this cup be taken from me. Yet not as I will, but as you will' (Matthew 26:39). This was not rebellion, nor a time when Jesus tried to twist God's arm and get out of doing the dishes. Instead – despite his clear agony – Jesus was submitting to God's rule and authority, saying 'not as I will, but as you will'. This is a key characteristic of Jesus's intimacy with God; he was so close that he was able to make two such extreme statements as 'Get me out of here' and 'I'll do it if you want'. It shows that he was able to be totally honest with God, refusing to gloss over any difficulties with pleasantries or denials. It also shows that he trusted God so much that he was able to walk into terrible torture, head held high telling the world that he trusted his Father. It wasn't just this one night of prayer that meant he was able to go through with the crucifixion – Jesus had been spending time with God for years before that – but it was this night that helped focus his mind and reassure him that what he was about to go through was all part of God's plan.

TALKING WITH GOD

Prayer is our method of communicating with God, just as it was the way Jesus communicated with him too. Through a passage in the book of Matthew we get to sneak up behind Jesus and find out what the exact ingredients are of successful prayer.

This, then, is how you should pray:

> Our Father in heaven,
> hallowed be your name,
> your kingdom come,
> your will be done,
> on earth as it is in heaven.
> Give us today our daily bread.
> Forgive us our debts,
> as we also have forgiven our debtors.

And lead us not into temptation,
but deliver us from the evil one.
(Matthew 6:9–13)

Jesus here gives us a model of how to pray to the Father by working through the following stages: beginning by praising God for who he is, what he has done and will do, we should then move on to praying for his work in the world, that it would keep moving on, spreading more of God's love and rule throughout the world. Next comes the time to pray for our own needs, and finally there is room to pray for help in our own daily struggles.

Through this style of prayer we get a picture that God wants a sense of balance to our prayer life. He doesn't just want a shopping list of items we require, nor should we feel that we cannot ask him for anything in the first place. After all, he loves to give good gifts, but if we are constantly begging or refusing to ask, it kind of gets in the way. The Lord's Prayer also shows us that we need to learn to find the balance between actively fighting the work of our enemy and being filled with the positive power of God. Most of all though, Jesus teaches us that we can call God 'Father'. Before he said this, no one would have dreamed of calling God anything other than Almighty, Holy One or a whole host of Hebrew names designed to express the many wonderful and majestic sides of God's character. From this point on, though, things were different: things were personal.

There's another fantastic prayer that we manage to listen in on later in the Bible. In the book of John, Jesus – on the verge of being arrested – prays for his disciples. He tells God about how he has taught them according to God's instruction, how they believed that Jesus was who he said he was. 'All I have is yours, and all you have is mine,' he says in John 17:10. This language reminds us of a wedding ceremony, and the expression of sacrifice is no accident. It is true: everything that Jesus had was God's; he and his Father were one. In that sense we, as his children, can agree with what Jesus said, perhaps even being bold enough to say to God ourselves, 'Everything that we have comes from you, and belongs to you.'

Before we get too carried away and reduce this line to the status of 'nice and cosy verse' (the kind that we repeat only when things are going well or we need cheering up), we must be careful not to miss out on the *huge* implications that lie at the heart of it. By following the first bit with 'and all you have is mine' Jesus turned up the heat and made it much more than a statement of how good God is at providing for us. He held out his hands and said with boldness, 'There is nothing you won't give me.' His Father gave him the key to the cupboard and told him to take his pick.

LISTENING TO GOD

This intimacy was not a one-way thing. There are times in the Bible when it seems as though God is so in love with his Son that he just cannot contain himself. As Jesus was baptised by John, God shouted down from heaven, saying, 'I love you, Son, and I'm totally proud of you.' This picture of God as the ultimate doting dad makes us smile – and so it should. We need to be clear that as well as the responsibility of following God, there is also a fantastic sense of joy and love around. God loves us, and when we get in touch with him and start to get to know him, there are often times when, again, he has trouble containing himself. After all God *is* love – and there's nothing wrong with enjoying the way he shows and shares it.

Luke 9 is interesting, if a little strange. Jesus has taken Peter, John and James with him up a mountain to pray, when suddenly he starts to look a little different. The sleepy disciples are jolted awake to find Jesus – his clothes now looking like a flash of lightning – has been joined by two other men, Moses and Elijah. These two greats of the Old Testament appear 'in glorious splendour', and speak with Jesus about his death (or 'departure' as Luke calls it). As the two visitors are leaving, Peter comments that he is glad he has seen it and then suggests that they put up some sort of memorial to mark the occasion. Just then God does another of his shouting down from heaven tricks, this time telling them that Jesus is his Son and that they should listen to him.

This passage has plenty to tell us about how to have an intimate relationship with God. The first and most obvious point is about the importance of prayer: Jesus and the three disciples took themselves off to pray. They made time for it, and obviously put in a fair old amount of effort to get in the mood by climbing up a mountain. We don't know what they were praying, but I think we can take a wild guess and assume that they weren't all asking for Jesus's face to go all shiny and for two key historical figures to show up for a chat. Because of that, we have to conclude that this amazing experience was all God's idea, which is not too out of keeping for him, especially when you consider many of the ways that he appeared to certain people throughout the Old Testament (burning bushes and all that). God loves two-way communication; he loves whispering to us so quietly that we have to get as close to him as we can, so close that we can almost touch him.

Looking at the story from the disciples' perspective, it's not surprising that they felt a bit drowsy – it happened again in the garden of Gethsemane. We also can get droopy when it comes to relating to God. Sometimes we will literally fall asleep, but more often it's our hearts and minds that need a wake-up.

We can too easily have our focus taken away from the things that God is doing, and we sometimes choose to give in to physical needs instead of learning spiritual lessons.

However, I'm not here to have a go at the disciples, especially as they soon realised that what they had seen was a definite treat. Peter was right when he said, 'Master, it is good for us to be here', and without reminding ourselves of the spiritual essence of what is going on around us, we can often get bogged down by issues that are irrelevant. Even though it didn't last long, the disciples were on track when they worked out that God was involved.

Sadly they lost the plot a bit when they suggested setting up a memorial. It may sound ridiculous to us now, but we're all capable of making the same basic error in our Christian lives. What Peter was doing was confusing the need for action with the need for contemplation. Jesus was well into doing things – healing, preaching, casting out demons and feeding huge crowds – but he also knew when the time was right to sit down and enjoy God's presence. This was one of those times, and Peter's idea of calling in the builders was a little too hasty. We all need to find the balance between the doing and the being. We need to learn how to imitate Jesus's perfect harmony in this matter: if we don't, we run the risk of either ending up tired and faithless or fat and useless.

God hadn't finished, and spoke aloud to prove it. There seems to be a dramatic change in the attitudes of the disciples after this – they decide to keep the incident to themselves. What prompted this sudden change from being on the verge of telling the world to telling no one? Obviously it was God's voice that spoke only a few words: 'This is my Son whom I have chosen; listen to him.' I think that they had been taking things for granted. They had forgotten some of the majesty of Jesus and instead had got into the habit of working hard on the business of spreading the word. Sound familiar? Things haven't changed much in 2000 years, and we all struggle with finding the right sense of balance in our lives. Don't get me wrong: spreading the word is a crucial element of our Christian calling, but we do it best when it comes from a place of hanging out with Jesus and just listening to him. What God did was to remind the disciples of the power and majesty of his Son. They realised again just how they should be responding to him, and were reminded of the need for them to listen to what he said.

Pursuing a relationship with God that allows time for soaking up his love as well as doing what he wants means being intimate with him. If we manage to do that we will enter a new phase in our relationship with God – one modelled by Jesus himself. It will take time, prayer and study, but along the way we will be able to love more, to give more, to know about God's own love for us and for others as well as to begin to understand the secrets of his heart. At the end of the day it's all about copying Jesus – after all, nobody did it better.

3

Just Do It

OBEDIENT LIKE JESUS

Like most of us, I never really went in for obedience much when I was little. In time something must have changed, for I gradually lost my passion for winding up my parents, but there was a period when I was the king of 'Just Say No'. My heyday was when I was eight years old. Every trip out began with gentle and loving suggestions from my mum and ended up with me screaming in public places. I can remember seriously thinking that instead of agreeing to behave myself in the supermarket, it was much more sensible to sneeze over the loose vegetables. This thought had been fermenting in my head for some time, and on one trip when my mother seemed to have more shopping to do than usual in less time, I took my opportunity.

I had warmed up with a few failed attempts at

trolley surfing, and when Mum had told me to stop, I quietly moved on up the aisle. Sneezing had been on my mind so much that I had even worked out a plan; if I rubbed my face hard and then stared at a bright light the sneezes would come thick and fast (which, as any bogied kid knows, is precisely the best way for sneezes to come). What's more, if I focused my efforts on the cauliflowers, the results could be truly impressive. With so many crevices into which I could propel my snot, I knew that it was a challenge, but as I calmly prepared the sneezes, I was sure that I was up to the task. I was building up to some spectacular mucus coverage when one of the store workers told me to stop whatever it was I was up to. Now my mum had already told me to behave, and this added instruction just didn't agree with me. I turned towards him, puffed out my chest and made my 3½ foot body look as large and threatening as I could. Throwing back my head I sucked in as much air as possible, but at my furthest point back something went wrong and instead of my lungs filling with air I must have swallowed. As I whipped my head back towards the shop assistant I let out what I hoped would be an all-covering projectile sneeze gross enough to send him home early from work with severe trauma. Instead I viciously assaulted him with a high pitched burp. He laughed and I suddenly felt a lot smaller. Just then my mum came along and scooped me up, taking me off for a quick talking to round the back of the tinned soup section. Humiliated by my failure to follow through, I quietly agreed to do whatever she said.

Thankfully Jesus didn't need a dose of public humiliation or parental dressing down to make him obey. In fact, obedience was one of the great marks of Jesus's life; without it we wouldn't be here today, and we certainly wouldn't have the gift of eternal life in heaven.

We know that God sent Jesus down to earth to be the ultimate sacrifice that would pay for our sins. This was not a last-minute decision or some crazy idea that he regretted later. It was a clear and calculated plan that had been formed hundreds of years before Jesus's birth. How can we know this? The Bible is full of Messianic prophecies – sections that predict the coming of Jesus, the Messiah, and the life he would lead – and together they prove that God had the whole thing worked out in minute detail. They start with his birth, as Micah 5:2 predicts that he would be born in Bethlehem (fulfilled in the events of Matthew 2:1–6 and Luke 2:1–20) and Isaiah 7:14 foretells that he would be born to a virgin (fulfilled in Matthew 1:18–25 and Luke 1:26–38). The prophecies also point to the fact that he would be rejected by his own people (Isaiah 53:1, 3 and Psalm 118:22) which is recorded in Matthew 26:3,4, John 12:37–43 and Acts 4:1–

12, tried and condemned (Isaiah 53:8) which is also reported in Luke 23:1–25 and Matthew 27:1,2, and would end up sitting at God's right hand (prophesied in Psalm 110:1 and described in Mark 16:19 and Luke 24:50,51).

But so far these prophecies concentrate on the facts of Jesus's life instead of the decisions he made. Isaiah 53:7 predicts that he would be silent before his accusers, something which happens in Matthew 27:12–14, Mark 15:3–4 and Luke 23:8–10. Psalm 22:14–16 and 17 describe the fact that the Messiah will die by crucifixion, which is fulfilled in Matthew 27:31 and Mark 15:20,25. The prophets also predicted that the Messiah would die as a sacrifice for sin (Isaiah 53:5–12) which is covered by John 1:29 and 11:49–52 and Acts 10:43 and 13:38, 39, as well as the fact that he would be raised from the dead (Psalm 16:10 as fulfilled by Acts 2:22–32 and Matthew 28:1–10).

I'm sorry to shove all these verses at you, but do you see my point? Jesus knew that suffering lay in store for him – he knew he would die and he knew he would be in pain, but he never backed down. Jesus was obedient to the last and he made sure that he went through with the plan, following it in minute detail.

What is even more impressive is the fact that Jesus was not just acting of his own accord, carrying out an idea that he had dreamt up one rainy afternoon. It was God's decision to send him down, and God's idea that he end up on a cross. In this sense, Jesus really was obedient, as he was acting under the instruction of someone else. 'I only do what I see the Father do,' he told people. The fact that the Father had also made a huge sacrifice by sending his own Son to pay someone else's debt meant that this particular game of Simon Says was unlike any other ever played.

Of course, you might be wondering why he did this. Was he a pushover, bored or just keen on trying to please people? None of these suggestions are right, you'll be glad to know. The truth is that Jesus was obedient because he had such an intimate relationship with his Father. He was obedient because he loved. Talking to the disciples, Jesus told them how we Christians are the branches, he is the vine and his Father the gardener. He was happy that his Father loved him, and part of that love had meant trimming off any branches that didn't bear fruit. Jesus applied the same standard of love to his disciples – encouraging them to reach their potential. It involved him trimming some of their branches too, and meant that they had to be obedient to him in the same way that he was obedient to his Father. Later it would cost some of them their lives too, but while Jesus was alive, he made a point of giving them some simple commands: 'Love each other as I have loved you' (John 15:12). This word wasn't just for the disciples of Jesus's day, but for all who claim to follow him at any point in time. If we say that we love him, then we cannot get out of the fact that we have to love others in the same way that he loved us, the same way that God loved him. That means getting down to some serious obedience, sacrifice and radical living. It also means that lives will be changed, saved and turned around, as people are reunited with God.

If we're still in any doubt about the importance of doing what Jesus tells us, there's a final reminder in the form of: 'You are my friends if you do what I command' (John 15:14). Placing these two verses together highlights something interesting; that we don't just obey for the sake of it, but that as friends of Jesus we want to do what makes him happy. Jesus doesn't just let us off the hook with a simple command to love. OK, so in him love meant dying on a cross and living totally for others, but in us I suspect that there is a danger that we could water it down a little. Perhaps if it was left at 'love' we would be happy just to go around being nice to old ladies and not murdering anyone. The fantastic thing about Jesus was that he knew the way we work and understood that we needed to have things spelt out for us as clearly as possible. That's why he chucked in the bit about *doing* as well as loving, why he made it clear that he wanted something more than just the Pharisees' academic abilities, why he chose people who would put their lives on the line. Christianity is all about finding the balance between adoring him and displaying him, between worship and evangelism. Sadly we often miss out. This time Jesus makes it clear that love without action also misses the point. He wants us to copy his lifestyle – both the things he did and the attitudes that he held. He was in perfect loving harmony with God and was totally obedient to his will.

Even though it might be tough along the way, true obedience as Jesus modelled it will bring about massive transformations. It's important that we understand this and don't just think of being obedient as some pointless exercise that only manages to keep us out of mischief. Done the right way (and that means done the Christ way) obedience can change everything. It is not a passive or wimpy option, it's not the sort of thing that we ought to be slightly embarrassed about. It gives glory to God and brings us all a little bit closer home to him.

THE GREAT COMMISSION

Alongside this Great Commandment to love God and others comes something called the Great Commission. Just before he returned to heaven Jesus gave his disciples a list of jobs to do. We'll look at this in detail later on, but his final speech begins with the words 'go into all the world and make disciples'

(Matthew 28:19). This means that we are supposed to get on with the job of evangelism, telling and showing people about Jesus, whose instructions stand side by side with the commandment to get down to some serious worship.

So you see, worship and evangelism are the perfect partnership; they belong together. If we separate them they are both reduced to something less than they ought to be. These are both things that Jesus told us to do. If we are going to try and follow him then we need to take his instructions seriously. We cannot separate worship from evangelism because it goes against everything that Jesus taught. The trouble is that many of us have separated them. Many of us are passionate about the one and try and blag it with the other. We have hidden worship away in the Church and kicked evangelism out into the world.

Acts chapter 2 is a great example of people being obedient to Jesus's twin commands. In fact, it's such a great example that it doesn't just show the jobs getting done efficiently, but it makes it clear to us how the two of them complement (and even depend on) one another. On the day of Pentecost the Holy Spirit fell on the disciples in the upper room. The first response to the coming of the Spirit was worship. The disciples spilled out onto the street 'declaring the wonders of God' in many different languages. As they worshipped a crowd gathered and began to ask questions about what was happening. Peter got up and preached the first evangelistic sermon in the history of the Church. Isn't it interesting that the first evangelistic talk was essentially given to answer the questions raised by the worship of the Church? That is how it should be. Anointed, passionate, intimate worship is one of the best evangelistic tools we have. There is something about the fragrance of such worship that draws non-believers.

At Soul Survivor we have seen this in some of our work over the years. At the start of last summer, a group of girls started coming to our church, and eight of them became Christians. We asked them what it was about our services that attracted them and helped them on their journey to God. Obviously I was convinced that they'd say it was the teaching. Perhaps they found it not only amusing and informative, but eloquent, captivating and life changing. I was sure that a couple of them would be able to quote their favourite chunks of Pilavachi sermons, and maybe they even had some of my ideas embroidered onto pillows and handkerchiefs which they gave away as presents to their family.

I think I got it wrong. Instead of declaring themselves Pilavachists, they described the talks as 'too long' and even 'a bit boring'. I resisted the temptation to tell them that they needed to repent, and swallowed my pride as they carried on. What had impressed them was the devotion expressed in the worship. It wasn't just the atmosphere of the services or the lighting, décor or duration. It wasn't the fact that the guitars were distorted and the bass was fat and funky. What had got them was the content. They seemed to learn more doctrine from the worship than from my sermons. Can you believe it? I was shocked.

> Jesus Christ, I think upon your sacrifice;
> you became nothing, poured out to death.
> Many times I've wondered at your gift of life,
> and I'm in that place once again.

They sing this Matt Redman song to each other at school. My Pilavachi special illustrations have never made it to school. I'm jealous, but kind of pleased too.

Evangelism that does not come from a lifestyle of worship can be very mechanical and dry. Worship that does not result in witness can become a self-indulgent ritual which is boring and repetitive. If there is great rejoicing in heaven over one sinner who repents, then how much more should the salvation of souls affect our worship on earth. These are the basics that we need to obey, just as Jesus did.

REVIVAL THROUGH OBEDIENCE

We humans have a great knack for getting confused. We believed that the world was flat, that draining blood was good for you and that wearing luminous socks was cool. The list of embarrassments is embarrassingly long, and we in the Church have done our bit to add to it. Now I don't want this to come out all wrong, but I think we ought to admit that many of us in the Church were a bit mistaken a few years ago. At times I was right there in the middle of it, loving it and having a ball, but now it's time for the truth.

God is an active God. He loves to roll up his sleeves and get involved with his people. This has happened on many occasions throughout the history of the Church, and I for one pray that it will continue to happen in the future. We tend to call these times revivals, and they often result in people discovering new and astounding things about God's character, falling in love with him even more and going deeper in their relationship with him. One of the most recent of these happened in a city called Toronto on Canada's border with America. This movement within the Church ran throughout the middle and end bits of the 1990s, and started as people rediscovered the joy of being loved by God. For many of us that joy did not result in an ability or great desire to communicate what we had received to others. A lot of good things happened; people got closer to God and rediscovered a fire for him. But something else didn't happen; when we had got closer to God we didn't listen hard enough for his instructions, or if we did hear them, we weren't obedient. Instead of responding to Jesus's command of 'Go', we preferred the more gentle 'Come', chilling with God. We fancied the worship a lot more than we fancied the evangelism.

At the time there was a lot of talk about Revival, but I sometimes feel that not all of us have been completely sure what 'Revival' actually means. Revival at its simplest is defined as 'bringing back to life that which was dead or close to death'. In that sense the Church constantly needs reviving. But many of us have been blind to the fact that it had been happening over the years anyway. Festivals like Soul Survivor, Cross Rhythms and Summer Madness in Ireland regularly attracted thousands of young people who were ready to do business with God. That would have been unheard of twenty years ago. In Britain alone, the Alpha courses introduced hundreds of thousands of people to Christ for the first time. This is still going on today, and up and down the country we are still hearing of new initiatives in evangelism springing up which are working. The Church is recovering its passion for Jesus as expressed in worship, its passion for the lost as expressed in evangelism and God's heart for the poor both at home and abroad.

So revival was and is taking place, and yet we need more, much more. It just isn't enough to get a few thousand in here or a few thousand there. If we're going to see big time change, we need to be reaching millions with the news and love of Jesus. At the time it was definitely good that we were hungry for God and desperate to see him do something massive, but we still managed to get confused. We began to feel like revival was a thing which would drop out of the sky at a certain date. This meant that we lost sight of the fact that, actually, Christianity is all about Jesus, not about magic rain or quick fixes. Some of us felt as though if we prayed hard enough, God would one day open a window in heaven and spray revival spray into the atmosphere, like air freshener. As the mist wafted down, people would breathe it in and suddenly fall over at the power of God – instantly transformed into A grade mature Christians. I don't believe this attitude is either biblical or helpful. I know that on the day of Pentecost the disciples waited until the Holy Spirit was poured out before they began to witness, but Pentecost has happened: the Spirit has been outpoured, and we have been called to go.

Revival is Jesus; more of his love, presence, holiness and power. I get quite upset when we still hear more about revival than we do about Jesus. Someone once famously prayed, 'Lord, don't send revival, come yourself' – I like that prayer because it's what Jesus did when he walked the earth. He came down and he spread love, healing, salvation and forgiveness all over through the way he lived his life. It all came through him as a human, weak like the rest of us. The apostle Paul learned that 'God's power is made perfect in weakness' (2 Corinthians 12:9) and found out that the secret of a full life and effective ministry is getting his power in my 'jars of clay' (2 Corinthians 4:7). Back in biblical times they were a little short on high street banks, so anything of value was stored in the home. The clever ones didn't stash their wad in fancy vases that would get stolen straight away, but in the cheapo jars of clay that no respectable thief would have bothered with. Paul uses this picture to show that while we may feel like second-grade jars of clay, God puts the treasure of his life in us. God works through us, not alongside, near or around us. This is a partnership, and we have to see the part that God has given us to play.

There's another lesson to learn from that time in the 1990s. We were in danger of sitting back and waiting for this wonderful thing to happen to us before we got out and did anything ourselves. 'Revival is God's work,' some people thought. 'Best leave it all up to him.' People took trips out to America and Canada – to Pensacola and Toronto – to 'catch the fire' and take it home to their churches.

I was one of them and had a great time getting closer to God, but let's not kid ourselves: the idea of going across the ocean to get a blessing, holiness or power and then bring it back with us is kind of bizarre and not at all easy to defend from Scripture.

The lesson that we can learn from all this is that revival will not come when we go across the ocean but when we go across the street. When we go in weakness to our neighbours and try to communicate the love of God to them in a way that is costly and makes us vulnerable. The feeding of the five thousand should be our model: Jesus took the little the disciples had (five loaves and two fish) and blessed and gave thanks for it. He then gave it back to them and told them to feed the people. The miracle happened in the disciples' hands. As they obeyed in faith, God multiplied the food. The disciples did not wait until the bread and fish had become 5000 Big Mac meals before they obeyed. They did it on the spot, putting their obedience before their doubts.

Jesus says, 'Go.' Go now. Instead of looking for yet another blessing, we should look for ways that we can be a blessing. 'Give and it will be given to you, pressed down, shaken together, running over, it will be poured into your lap' (Luke 6:38). It's all part of a simple rule: go and give away what you've been given.

I have learned to my cost that if I have more input

(food) than output (exercise) I do not keep growing, I just get fat. Even though a lot of this was going on a few years ago, I am still worried that we in the Church could be in danger of getting fat. We need to exercise by getting on with the business of being obedient to what Jesus told us to do. That means serving the poor as we fight for social justice and as we seek to win the lost. We can learn from this though. We can decide that instead of catching half the message, we will look for the whole story. We know that God isn't just into sitting back and soaking up the easy vibes. He's a God of action as well as relationship – a God of such intense love that he cannot stand to have injustice carry on while his people are around.

He spelled it out for us through Jesus in Matthew 25; believe me, it doesn't get much clearer than this. In a story to his disciples in which he illustrates the final judgment every one of us must face, Jesus challenges those who are doomed to eternal torment: 'I was hungry and you gave me nothing to eat, I was thirsty and you gave me nothing to drink, I was a stranger and you did not invite me in, I needed clothes and you did not clothe me, I was sick and in prison and you did not look after me.'

The wretched souls protest: 'Lord, when did we see you hungry or thirsty or a stranger or needing clothes or sick or in prison, and did not help you?'

But Jesus's crushing reply is: 'Whatever you did

not do for one of the least of these, you did not do for me.'

4

Living in the Real World

OUT OF THE CHRISTIAN GHETTO

As well as having a supremely intimate relationship with the Father and being committed to obey him, Jesus's time on earth teaches us another lesson that should revolutionise the way we live. Wherever he went, whatever he did, Jesus was fuelled by compassion. He saw the sick and he healed them, met the oppressed and set them free, encountered a world living far away from God and showed us the way home. He didn't do it for an ego boost and he didn't do it 'cos he was bored. Jesus did it because it was as much a part of him as his heart and lungs – he wouldn't be Jesus without compassion.

So you won't be surprised when I say that if we want to graduate to wearing spiritual trousers we have to learn how to follow in the footsteps of the most compassionate man who ever lived. Again this isn't a cue for us to hit the panic button, as God is far more concerned about us being on the right tracks rather than at the end of the journey – we never could be a match for Jesus, but we can all have a go as he gives us his power to live.

As ever we hunt for clues in the Bible. Just looking at a list of whom Jesus talked with during his travels throws up some of the lowest and most despised members of society: a tax collector, an apparently insane hermit, a criminal, a poor widow, an adulterous woman, a sick woman, a blind beggar, an outcast with leprosy, a young girl, a traitor, a helpless and paralysed man, a woman from a foreign land, an enemy who hated him and a Samaritan woman. To each of them he preached the same message of love and acceptance, offering hope and salvation through himself.

There's a link that joins each of these people. They were on the edge. (Of course, you could easily argue that there was no Church when Jesus was around, and so everyone was on the edge, how then can we compare the two?) Still, we cannot ignore the fact that Jesus's most astounding and controversial acts – the ones that sent the biggest shock waves throughout society and did the most to turn it upside down – were performed in the midst of sinners. After all, I think it's kind of logical: if imitating Jesus's life is like shining a light, where will it appear brightest, surrounded by other lights or on its own in the darkness?

The fact is that we cannot truly copy Jesus's compassionate lifestyle unless we copy it in similar locations, which is why we need to take an honest look at how we relate to the world.

I was in South Africa once when I started to get a little distressed. I wasn't worried about the usual things – too much rain and not enough curry – instead, this time I was getting stressed about the Church. It seemed to me that the white Christian community out there was enjoying a culture all of its own, as if it was happy to be completely separated from the rest of the world. What they had set up was a ghetto, where everything that was going on in the world was being washed down, cleaned up and blandly duplicated ready for consumption by the Christian community.

I heard plenty of teaching out there, too. I heard many people tell young Christians not to drink alcohol, go to nightclubs or listen to any non-Christian music. All these things were the devil's own, and good Christian kids should stay away, choosing instead a diet of Contemporary Christian Music (CCM if you're into the jargon), church events and Fanta.

I saw how all the people had acted on this message, and I was horrified at the result. What was produced was a Christian community that was happy hanging around with itself. They had their own little parties, with their own Christian friends where they listened to their own Christian radio stations which played their own Christian music. They were separated from the world. They were separated from people outside the Church. It reminded me of biblical times, but more of the professional religious men than of Jesus.

One day when I was feeling brave or stupid (depending on how you look at it) I gave a talk. I told people how I thought it was a good thing to listen to non-Christian music. I said that I thought music that wasn't written by Christians was often much better, that I thought it was good to go to nightclubs. I finished up by telling them that I don't think drinking alcohol sends you to hell.

The following Sunday, the pastor of one of the churches in Durban got up and said to the young people, 'I've been told that someone has come into our city and told you that it's OK to listen to non-Christian music and go to nightclubs. I want to tell you, that is trash.' That was quite a shock. I don't know why I was surprised, I suppose I had hoped that by saying what I had said people would see the sense. Instead, it made certain ones out there get kind of agitated.

Back home in England we struggle with many of the same things and face similar issues. Isn't it strange that I had to go to the other side of the world to realise that many of us in the Church think of holiness not first of all as obedience to God but as being separate from the world. We're not really talking about music, clubs or booze here, but instead are examining something at the heart of our beliefs. Now I love South Africa and all the Christians I've met out there, but I think some had got the wrong end of the stick. What Jesus preached about holy living never prevented him from taking his love out to the people that needed it most. Holiness is a tool, a blueprint for how we should live our lives. As well as knowing what to avoid, true holiness is following God. Our misunderstandings come from the fact that we have signed up for a model of holiness that we see in the Israel of the Old Testament where they were constantly struggling to avoid being contaminated by the other nations and their false gods. Jesus gave us another model. He was the first missionary; he came to contaminate the world with his love and power – that's why we see him spending time with the 'publicans and sinners', the prostitutes, the tax collectors, the Samaritans and all those whom the religious leaders saw as people to avoid.

Here in the UK we have got confused about holiness and compassion, and we still tend to regard holiness as something that keeps us apart from the world, as opposed to something that keeps the world out of us. When he was around in first-century Israel, Jesus encountered the same things I saw in South Africa. The Pharisees and the teachers of the law kept trying to trip him up with the laws about not touching this or that and not healing on the Sabbath.

What they were pushing for was for Jesus to say that we shouldn't get involved, not with tax collectors, not with sinners and certainly not with women in the middle of their menstrual cycle. Jesus was touched by a woman who was bleeding. She was healed. Lepers were unclean, not just physically but spiritually as well, but Jesus touched them and they were healed. Respectful Jews regarded prostitutes as untouchables but Jesus cared for them, forgave them and loved them.

Jesus was a man on a mission. In a sense he redefined holiness. Holiness for Jesus was not about the display of knowledge of the law, it was about the passion of the heart, and Jesus's heart beats loud and strong for a certain type of person. He went to the places that respectable religious people wouldn't go, and he managed to go there and still live a holy life. He went to a place where there were drunks and he didn't get drunk. He went to a place where there were sexual sinners and yet he didn't sin sexually. He went with tax collectors and sinners and partied with them, and yet lived a holy life that managed to be so attractive that people responded to him completely. When he went to all these places, he didn't go just to test his willpower, to see if he really could manage to resist temptation. Instead, he went because he was pushed by a deep and violent urge within him. We call it compassion, and Jesus was full of it. It affected his life in every detail – from whom he talked with to how he chose to die. Jesus acted because he loved the people that God had created, and he could not stand idly by and see them suffer without him.

In Luke 19 we read about Jesus travelling to Jericho as the crowd were lining the streets to see him. A very small tax collector called Zacchaeus climbed a tree so that he could get a good look. Now the point about Zac is that he was a social outcast; he worked for the Romans and defrauded his own people. Jesus, seeing him up the tree, says something stunning: 'Zacchaeus, come down immediately. I must stay at your house today.' As a result of those words Zac turned his back on all that he had done wrong. Jesus's words immediately undid a lifetime of self-doubt and shame. Jesus told Zacchaeus that he was worth spending time on, regardless of how bad his business ethics were. We need to learn to be fired by that same compassion – a sort that works outside of church. We can't go on spending our lives retreating from the world into the Church, getting scared at the slightest thing that challenges our faith. We mustn't retreat into our little ghettos, because if we do we may never get out. We've got to get out in the real world and live life to the full as God's people, holy, pleasing to him, fired up by a desire to follow God's lead and spread his love in the midst of a broken and hurting world. 'Get ready,' we need to say to the culture, 'we're coming to your house.'

Sometimes I worry about all our Christian

subculture stuff; we've got our own Christian record labels, bookshops, magazines and festivals. We're involved in all of these at Soul Survivor, and I know that each of these can do great things for God, yet the flip side to all that we have built up around the Church is that sometimes these things can create a Christian subculture, a Christian ghetto where we retreat from the world, a place where we don't understand what the world is thinking.

TRUE COMPASSION

Jesus's first miracle was turning water into wine at a wedding feast in Cana (John 2:1–11). He didn't do it as a publicity stunt; he went to the party to enjoy himself. He performed the miracle to make people happy, not only to demonstrate his power and glory. Even more intriguing is the fact that the only people who knew about it were the servants. If you want to see the miracles, be a servant.

There's a Christian lady called Jackie Pullinger. She's written books and has been in the public eye for many years, but neither of them are the reason why she is well known and widely respected. She used to live inside Hong Kong's notorious Walled City – a horrendous slum (thankfully no longer in existence) where society at times seemed to be breaking down in front of her very eyes. She lived surrounded by drug dealers and addicts, prostitutes and gang members, Aids victims and orphans. She worked with anyone who wanted help – offering care and the chance to rebuild a broken life. As a result hundreds of people have become Christians through her work, she has helped to turn a city around and has saved lives, all because of the compassion that she's received from Jesus.

I heard her speak once. She flew over from Hong Kong landing at Heathrow at 6.00 a.m. She spoke at 10.00 a.m. and again at 2.00 p.m. and then caught the 10.00 p.m. flight back to Hong Kong. Not even time for a shop at Harrods. Lots of people came to listen to her talk about the things that were on her mind, and her message was uncompromising. She was clear and straight up in the way that only someone who is actually doing what she says can be. I suppose that was one reason why I found it so shocking. I know this is corny, but she really did remind me of Mother Teresa. I never heard Mother T speak, but I know that she had a knack of cutting through all the complications we make and telling it as it is. This was how Jackie spoke; she was blunt, simple and uncompromising. A little bit like Jesus, I suppose.

Jackie talked about living a life of compassion and service. She talked about sacrifice. She talked about losing your life to find it. She told us how she and the rest of her team had heard about something that was going on back in western churches in 1996. They had heard that Christians in some place had started laughing and falling over. (This seemed kind of strange to them but I don't think they paid it too much attention.) Later she heard that Christians had started flying out to visit this place full of laughter, spending cash on airfares and staying in hotels just to catch the laughter for themselves. It all sounded like a bit of a party, and Jackie and the rest were a bit confused. But they prayed, 'OK, Holy Spirit, your people really need to rediscover the joy of their salvation and it is good that that they can take aeroplanes to the laughing. But because this is you, Holy Spirit, after they have taken the aeroplanes to the laughing, some of them will also take aeroplanes to the dying and the crying.'

Jackie stopped telling her story for a while, looking around her.

'And we waited,' she said, 'but you didn't come.' It wasn't as though she was angry – it seemed much more like she was confused by the whole thing.

I was very upset. You see, I've been to Toronto. Twice. On the other hand I've never been much into the Bangladesh blessing. I was cross. How dare someone make a day trip to England to lecture us on how to live our lives? Who does she think she is? She doesn't have any idea about the situation in the British Church. My response was a little bit like that of a Pharisee, I suppose.

The response in others was very interesting. Those

who were more mature in years reacted very similarly to me, and it took a while to really understand what she said. The younger ones, however, were in no doubt. They were up the front for ministry, repenting of the fact they had not been giving more of their pocket money to relieve world suffering. They were ready to book their one-way tickets to Hong Kong. As I looked at them and saw how fired up they were, I realised that I am getting old. There was a time when I would have been up there with the best of them, ready to go at a moment's notice for Jesus. Now I have a church and ministry to support. I have responsibilities and commitments. Mortgages have to be paid. Books have to be written. Such is life.

Friends of mine were telling me how the teenagers in their family came back from their youth meeting passionate about how they were going to change the world for Jesus. The change was going to take place in the next few weeks, but they were just wondering whether they should start the international ministry before or after their GCSEs? The parents had just finished their homegroup meeting where one of the members had asked for prayer so he would have the courage to at last tell his work colleagues that he went to church. I've been a bit like that lately – looking for the small things instead of letting my heart beat wildly with God-given compassion.

In becoming worldly wise (cynical) have I lost the passion that results in reckless behaviour, like walking on the water? Have I lost the compassion that leads to a holy boldness, the sort that tears a hole in a roof so that a paralysed friend can be healed (Mark 2:1–12)? We see in the book of Joshua that Caleb was an old man with a young man's heart. He saw with the eyes of faith. He ran the last lap of his life as if it was the first.

I know that this isn't just about physical age – God is not just a God of the young any more than he is just a God of the old. His compassion is compatible with all of us, and all we have to do is keep the fire burning in our hearts and to work it out in our lives. As I have found, to realise that you have lost something is the first step to finding it again. Let us not settle. The first line of a children's song says 'It's an adventure, following Jesus'. Don't lose the sense of adventure. Don't quit. Let us not grow weary. Let's change the world with that same brand of holy compassion that started the whole thing off.

Having compassion means that we need to be a people of our culture, as well as a people who know how to stand counter to the culture in certain areas. We need to be in the middle of it, dishing out love and truth and being genuine and honest with people, but there are certain things that we need to take a stand against. For example, when it comes to greed – something which our culture is full of – our voices need to be heard. That doesn't mean escaping from the culture in order to be generous in our own little clique, but instead being generous right in the middle of the greedy culture: that's where the light shines brightest. Let's be sexually pure in the midst of a culture where there isn't purity. Let's be responsible in a culture where people get off their heads. That is what compassion is – being like Jesus when he met with the prostitute who poured a year's wages' worth of perfume over his feet (John 12:1–8). He didn't slip or stumble, he remained pure and holy, having mercy on her when no one else would even give her any respect. His compassionate heart was big enough to forgive her for her sinful lifestyle.

Many of us are afraid to really engage with our culture because of a fear of contamination. We are afraid to get out there and put our faith on the line, showing love in the darkest places. Perhaps we are worried that our faith won't hold out, perhaps we worry that we haven't got what it takes and that the radical obedience to Jesus's command of spreading the news is best left to the brave ones like Jackie Pullinger. Perhaps we are right to be scared and aware of the danger that faces us; moving out takes us away from all the religious comforts that we have built up around us. But it simply isn't an option to stay in the cosy warmth of the Church, for how can we show the full outrageous and powerful extent of God's compassion in there? We need to wake up to the fact that we have a spirituality that only works in the Church. That cannot be right, we need to relearn and to find a spirituality that works in the world. For it is God's world, and he loves it. We need to be committed to his world, to be part of his world. It's called incarnation, and it's what God did when he became a human being and lived among us as Jesus. A Jesus spirituality works in the world. Do we believe the Scripture that says, 'he that is in us is greater than he that is in the world' (1 John 4:4)? John 1:14 says, 'The word became flesh and made his dwelling among us.' In *The Message* version of the Bible that particular passage is paraphrased 'and Jesus moved into the neighbourhood'. I love that. We need to be like Jesus: God's representatives in the midst of his broken and hurting world.

5

The Desert

WHY ME?

To be brutally honest, I'd much rather spend the next few pages talking about luxury desserts than spiritual deserts – given the choice, a Triple Chocolate Fudge Walnut Cream Surprise beats intense loneliness and testing any day – but somehow I don't think it would be that useful a chapter. You see we all go through times when Christianity is tough. Instead of being vibrant and full of life, it seems grey, God seems distant and the faith that once had you feeling on top of the world suddenly seems to have run dry. As Christians we call them Desert Times (more on why we call them that later), and they are no more a sign that your faith is weak than the 'Virtually Fat Free' label on the Triple Chocolate Fudge Walnut Cream Surprise means that what lies inside is good for you.

Comforting as that news might be, it can

sometimes seem like small consolation when we are actually in the middle of one of these difficult times. When God seems a million miles away, when we're convinced that he's about as interested in us as we are in prayer, it can be hard not to start getting on a bit of a downer about things. After all, when we feel as though we've either been conned, stood up or simply rejected outright, getting ourselves motivated again can seem like an impossible task.

The reason why I can be so presumptuous by including a chapter like this is because difficult times are a natural part of the Christian life. As I said, we *all* go through it, and not only when we are in our early days of getting to know God. These experiences crop up all the way throughout even the longest Christian life; in fact they are actually a vitally important part of the Christian life: not only do they help us put into perspective the mind-numbingly great times that we all enjoy every now and then, but they also teach us one of the most valuable lessons that Christianity ever has to offer: perseverance.

I know that dropping a word like perseverance into a book like this is dumb, but the point is that it's true. Persevering, deciding to stick with it despite the fact that you feel as though you're stumbling about like a zombie is the key to growing up in your relationship with God.

There's a famous story in the Bible that Jesus told. It concerns a rich master who, just before a lengthy trip away, calls three of his servants together and hands them different amounts of cash. He tells each of them to get on with the business of making more cash out of what's in their hands, and goes away. When he returns he calls each of them in and asks to see what they've done with his wad. It turns out that the two who had been given the larger sums had managed to double their purses. The master is happy, but the smile goes when the third servant arrives and tells him that because he thought the master was such a hard man, he stuck the cash in a hole in the ground and had managed to increase its value by absolutely nothing at all.

This story – you can read it for yourself in Matthew 25 – is normally used to illustrate the fact that we all have talents from God that we ought to be using for him. I happen to think that it also can take a slightly different spin: the need for perseverance. Think about the servant – the one who made no profit and did nothing while his master was away. He buried the coin and, presumably, forgot all about it. The clever servants, however, had a different story to tell. Instead of forgetting about things, they carried on, working hard at increasing their return, despite the fact that their master was nowhere to be found. He was unavailable for either advice or reassurance. There must have been times when it looked as though they were about to lose everything – such is the nature of money – and at those times I am sure that they would have been tempted to give up on the whole idea. Instead, though, they carried on, receiving their master's pleasure when he returned.

This is how it should be with us. When God seems far away we too have a choice; either we bury our faith and forget about the Master, or we continue in his absence, carrying out the orders that he has given us until we feel close to him again.

But, you may just be about to ask, how can we be sure that we *will* feel close to him again? In the dark night of the soul, daylight seems a long way off, and nothing can seem certain. Remember how I said that you weren't alone? It's not just Christians today who have been through it, but believers and followers of God throughout history. The Bible is generously seasoned with stories of people who feel as though God is playing an elaborate game of hide and seek with them. In a sense he is; he takes away his presence, his nearness, from them and asks them a simple question: will you search for me?

This is exactly what happened to Moses. Having left the comfort of the palace he found himself in the wilderness for quite some time before his run-in with God in the shape of the burning bush. The same thing happened to the rest of his countrymen a few years later as they spent forty years wandering around the desert trying to find the promised land. This was not necessarily due to the fact that the promised land was a particularly long way away, but more due to their desperate need to rediscover their relationship with God before they rebuilt their society.

Later on in the Bible we hook up with Elijah (1 Kings 17) – surely one of the nuttiest prophets in the whole book. Reading the story it can seem as though his life is a string of easy miracles, joined together by fireproof faith and an almost constant hotline to God. But look closer and it's possible to see the difficult times in there too. When Elijah called a drought, the Lord told him to go and hide at a place called the Kerith ravine and later to another place called Zarephath, both of which were in the desert. Elijah spent three years there, with only a widow and her son for company. Think about that for a while, and it becomes clear that those years were no picnic. In those days, being in the desert or the wilderness meant constant danger and a daily struggle for food. Add to that the absence of any miracles, and we can be sure that Elijah would have had to work hard to keep on track with God. What happens next leads us to the inevitable conclusion that he must have done OK, as he kicked butt on the hugest scale by defeating the prophets of Baal on top of Mount Carmel.

These stories are not confined to the Old Testament either, as Jesus's coming changed little about this natural rhythm of relationship with God Almighty. We'll go into this even more later on, but briefly we know that John the Baptist did his proclaiming about Jesus from the literal desert, and that

Jesus too spent forty days on his own.

As we're in the mood for metaphor, let's think about the physical characteristics of these desert and wilderness places. Essentially, they are barren – free from virtually all signs of life – as well as being dry. It is a fight just to find water and survive. Third, they are always inhospitable places, being low on the natural resources that we rely on for comfort. If this is equally true of the spiritual deserts and wildernesses that we all visit from time to time, then the obvious question that springs to mind is why? Why, when God is loving and kind, would he ever want us to go through experiences that seem so destructive?

The book of Deuteronomy answers exactly that question. Having been asked it by the Israelites, the Lord answers.

Remember how the Lord your God led you in the desert these forty years, to humble you and to test you in order to know what was in your heart, whether or not you would keep his command. (Deuteronomy 8:2)

BEING HUMBLED

The first thing that is on God's agenda for our difficult times is the process of our being humbled. I know that this works for me because whenever I am not struggling with a desert experience, when life is cushy and everything seems to be working out well, I can start to think that I've got something to do with it. Then I can get around to thinking that I'm self-sufficient, that I can handle life, I can handle ministry, I can handle just about anything that gets thrown at me. I'm not alone in this, and whenever we prosper, there are many of us who start to self-inflate our own sense of importance. By sending us into the desert places, by showing us that we certainly do not have the Midas touch, God offers us the chance of realising the truth: that apart from him we can do nothing of any value.

It wasn't that long ago that I went through my latest – and possibly 'greatest' – rough time. When I first realised that God no longer seemed so close I started to panic. Was this the end of everything, I thought. Was I losing my faith? Which of my secret sins was it because of? Had God taken his anointing away? Was it ever there in the first place? I went through this usual list of doubts and panics, each of which felt intensely real at the time.

It came to a bit of a climax on Easter Day. I was standing at the front of church trying to lead the meeting, but inside my head was nothing but a panic about what to do next. I had no idea what to do, and absolutely no idea of what God wanted. This was serious, and the feelings of nervousness and panic made the experience far more intense than anything I had gone through in a long while. Of course I tried not to show it, and acted in a most professional manner, but inside was the cry of 'Lord, I don't hear a thing. Help.' I left the meeting with a very real sense of sorrow and pain inside – it had been the culmination of weeks of feeling spiritually alone, and I felt terrible.

Looking back now I can see that before things had started to seem a little stale I had got used to having God's voice on tap, so much so that I had begun to cut corners. Where previously I might have prayed long and hard about a certain decision, I had started to wing it, trusting in God's abilities as a quick fix supplier. I'd been neglecting the relationship and seemed to be suffering the consequences. The thing about going through a desert experience is that you cannot cut corners – they simply are not there to cut. The only options open are either to ignore God or to pursue him – and even then, pursuing him can for a while feel like a wild goose chase.

Despite this – in fact because of this – God humbles us in the desert, stripping us of all our supports. He allows us to stand there and to say, 'Unless you send the rain, I'm going to die of thirst, unless you send manna, I've got nothing to eat.'

LEARNING ABOUT OURSELVES

The second result to force its way out of the whole deal is a rigorous testing of what is in our hearts. Through the revelation of brutal truth about our attitudes and feelings each of us finds out what we are really like. While it may be quicker for God to hand the information to us in the form of a nicely typed and bound personality profile, somehow I don't think we would take things to heart. Instead God uses real life to get our attention and teach the lessons. I'm glad of this because sometimes I can kid myself that emotionally and spiritually things are a lot better than they actually are. Things on the outside can be going well enough that admitting difficulties or even looking at yourself becomes a bit of a non-starter. But of course, as soon as you're in the desert, when the distractions of things going well are a distant memory, looking in at yourself is one of the few things you *can* do. Poor old Moses had to put up with forty years of building sandcastles in the desert with the whingeing Israelites. The dramatic change that needed to take place – the acceptance of the Israelites of God as the one true God – meant that the whole thing took so long. There's no point expecting a desert experience to last half an hour, you may as well be at the seaside for all the good it will do you.

Numbers are significant in the Bible. Seven

represents God's perfection, three represents God (as Trinity) and forty seems to get used whenever the writer wants to imply that a large period of time has passed. For example, the point isn't that Jesus spent exactly forty days in the wilderness, but that he was out there for a long time. The same goes for the amount of time it rained during the great flood and the length of time that the Israelites spent wandering and whingeing on their way to the promised land. God understands the value of time, and knows that through the passing of large chunks of it, he can test our hearts.

As well as testing us by making us face up to the truth about ourselves, God also uses desert experiences to refine us, to show up our faults and encourage us to put them behind us. In the early 1990s a bunch of people from Kansas City started coming over and travelling around churches in the UK. These people were all incredibly gifted in the prophetic side of things, and at some point I got it into my head that as soon as they saw people they knew everything they were thinking. When I heard they were coming to my church I was a tad confused. On the one hand I was desperate to see some spot-on prophesying get done, but on the other I was scared that the minute I walked in the door they were going to reveal my most secret of sins to the whole congregation. Having decided to go I made sure that I was ready. For three and a half hours I crawled around my flat on my knees, desperately repenting for any sin I had committed as well as any sin that I might have contemplated committing.

I came out of the meeting with my reputation intact as well as having seen some amazing things, but it was only a few weeks later that I understood how God had spoken to me directly too. I realised that we don't need to wait for the prophet to reveal the things that are wrong in us, in the same way that we don't need to wait for the big meeting before we get down to some honest confession. Instead the good old desert time offers each of us a chance to face up to the truth about ourselves. Deserts offer a quiet alternative to the noise and bustle that we create around us when everything is going according to plan.

The Bible draws out this theme in Deuteronomy 8:

When you have eaten and are satisfied [when I give you manna in the desert], praise the Lord your God for the good land he has given you. Be careful that you do not forget the Lord your God, failing to observe his commands, his laws and his decrees that I am giving you this day. Otherwise, when you eat and are satisfied, when you build fine houses and settle down, and when your herds and flocks grow large and your silver and gold increase and all you have is multiplied, then your heart will become proud, and you will forget the

Lord your God, who brought you out of Egypt, out of the land of slavery. (vv. 10–14)

I tell you what, the Bible beats Freud for human psychology any day of the week. Isn't what this describes exactly what happens? When God prospers us and seems to make everything go well, we must remember to praise him. If we don't adopt the habit of worship, that habit of giving thanks even when there doesn't appear to be a lot to be thankful for, then when we eventually do come to the place of prosperity we lose the plot entirely and forget the Lord our God. The practice phase always starts in the desert, when there is less at stake. Once we have shown that we can keep going with God, then he trusts us with more.

THE DESERT FOR OUR OWN GOOD

In Luke chapter 4 the writer covers the phase of Jesus's life soon after he has been filled with the Holy Spirit in the River Jordan. Having been filled he gets led by the Spirit into the desert, where for forty days he is tempted by the devil. I find it interesting that Luke makes a point of telling us that the first thing the Holy Spirit did once he was hooked up with Jesus was to lead him into the desert. I don't know about you, but when I think there's a danger of me being led into the desert, I generally run the other way and do anything possible to avoid it.

But thankfully Jesus was not like me, and he allowed himself out of obedience to be led there. I don't think he went kicking and screaming either; I imagine that he was a willing son, prepared to do whatever it took to bring on the revelation of the goodness and faithfulness of the Creator God. Despite the devil's varied attempts at getting Jesus to give in to temptation, Jesus saw straight through him and answered him by quoting God's word from Scripture.

We too can learn to hear God's word more clearly when things in life are not going so well. It is important to remember that all is not lost forever – desert experiences only ever last for a specific season. If you can use them as a chance to stick your teeth into your faith, then the staleness will always give way to something much better. When Jesus returned from the desert – after God had allowed him to go through all that he needed him to go through – Luke makes it clear to us that he returned on top form: 'He returned to Galilee in the power of the Spirit.' Some of us love being filled by the Spirit, but if we're honest, we lack the sense of direction and purpose that accompanied Jesus's Spirit-filled return. Perhaps we get ourselves in these ruts because we gladly accept the Spirit's first introduction but resist the lead to follow him into the desert.

The main reason behind these difficult experiences

can be found tucked away in the book of Hosea. Through the prophet God says. 'Therefore I am now going to allure her; I will lead her into the desert and speak tenderly to her' (Hosea 2:14). He leads us into the desert places too so that we will fall in love with him again.

The Song of Songs is one of the most unusual books in the whole Bible. If the censor had to put a classification on it, it would definitely be an 18. It's the story of a love affair between a king and a young lady, and traditionally Christians have taken it as a picture of Jesus's relationship as the King with us, his Church, as the young lady. In chapters 1 and 2 we see the lover wooing the young lady, which is followed by this in chapter 3:

> All night long on my bed
> I looked for the one my heart loves;
> I looked for him but did not find him.
> I will get up now and go about the city,
> through its streets and its squares;
> I will search for the one my heart loves.
> So I looked for him but did not find him.
> The watchmen found me
> as they made their rounds in the city.
> 'Have you seen the one my heart loves?'
> Scarcely had I passed them
> when I found the one my heart loves.
> I held him and would not let him go

till I had brought him to my mother's house,
to the room of the one who had conceived
  me.

(vv. 1–4)

This is a desert experience. They had been close,
spending part of the evening together tenderly ex-
changing expressions of love, but then he disappears,
playing hide and seek. She realises what she's missing
and is unable to sleep at night, so she gives up the
comfort of her bed and wanders around the deserted
city searching for him. Eventually when she finds
him, in her joy she holds him and does not let him go.
She takes him to the most intimate place of all: the
bedroom of the one who conceived her. The desert is
a place where the Lord plays hide and seek for a
while. He asks us – will we forsake our comforts and
search for him? The desert's the place where we find
out how much we love him.

  It worked for the people who followed Moses, and
it still works for us today. When we are stripped of
everything else that would give us comfort, everything
else that would meet our emotional and sometimes
physical needs, we come back and fall in love with
Jesus all over again.

6

Heart for the Lost

LOVING AS GOD LOVES

It took me a long time to realise that Christianity
was more than a collection of rules and regulations.
When I was fifteen I decided never to sin again. It
didn't work. When I was seventeen I worked out that
if I stuck enough 'Jesus – He's the real thing' stickers
on immovable objects around Harrow, the second
coming would be just around the corner. It wasn't.
At the age of twenty-seven I was convinced that all I
had to do to win God's love was set up and run a
successful open youth group on my own, converting
hundreds of ex-offenders along the way. I was wrong.

Thankfully in the middle of all my mess-ups,
wrongs turns and false starts I've discovered that
God is no way near as obvious as we think he is.
Instead of wanting to create an army of immaculate
soldiers, I suspect that he would be a lot happier with

a bunch of passionate and wild warriors. Put another way, God looks for the hidden treasure instead of the printed map. He's not solely after our doing great things for him (even though that is a wonderful aim), because all the spectacular deeds in the world count for little if we don't have the relationship with the Father.

Now that word 'relationship' might cause us a few problems. Are we to assume that we need to 'pull' God? (Not quite.) Do we just dump him when things get a little bit heavy? (Ideally not.) Does God want us to get to know him? (A definite yes.) You see, while it's not a carbon copy of them, relationship with God does have more to do with human relationships than we think. In fact, we've done ourselves and God no favours by separating in our minds the spiritual from the physical. We've put God in a box along with Sunday services, giving to charity and feeling bad. All the rest of our lives – the work, the romance, the pain and the bodily functions – we've stored well away from him. That's a shame, especially as God created us to experience and enjoy those things in the first place.

Any relationship is only as good as the communication that exists between two people. Sadly there are too many marriages around where both sides are so caught up with the minute details, the daily jobs and chores that sit at the front of their minds that they never really *talk*. The image of the tired dad coming home and slouching down in front of the TV for the duration of the evening has become so common that it hardly raises a smile. Talking, expressing ideas, hope, pain and sadness is the key to building strength in any relationship. Without it, not only do we miss out on getting to the heart of someone, but we are kept up on the surface where things soon get stale and dry.

This can happen with God. OK, so he may not be the TV dinner type, but if we don't commit ourselves to spending decent time with him, then we too can miss out on the prize of getting close to him, hearing what he has to say. Having a relationship with God means hooking up with him, downloading data straight from his heart. It means spending time with him and sussing out exactly what it is that gets him excited and sad. It means being real, being honest with him about the good and the bad. Developing our relationship with God is always on the agenda for us Christians, and in a way this whole series of books is designed to help us go further on and further in.

But hold on: as soon as you start moving in towards God you discover something strange. Just as you think you're going to cosy down with him, enjoying some one-on-one chat and niceness, God turns you around and sends you straight back out again. This is not due to a sudden fit of bad temper from God or bad breath from you, but due to the plain and simple truth that belongs at the heart of Christianity: God's heart is for the lost. Put in English, that means that God loves the poor, the oppressed and the lonely. He loves the underdog and is mighty keen that we step in line and follow his lead. He wants us to get out there just like he did, finding the people who don't know him and bringing them back on home where they belong. God's heart is for the lost.

PASSION FOR THE POOR

But how, you may ask, do we know what to do? Simple, comes the answer: just look at how God has got involved in the lives of his people. When the time came for God to make camp on earth by specifically choosing a nation to be known as *his* people, he made an interesting selection. If I were doing the picking I would have gone out and found the most talented, ferocious, cultured and intelligent people around. I would have picked the Greeks. They would have been brilliant, reflecting all the bits of my even more brilliant character.

Thankfully I'm not God. When it came to decision time God had one crew at the top of his list: the Israelites. They were the lowest of the low, slaves to a cruel race (the Egyptians). They were routinely beaten and killed, and were unable to stand up for themselves when Pharaoh decided to kill all the firstborn males. Calling them poor is an understatement, as their lack of cash was probably the last of their worries. They were the victims of oppression on a scale that we cannot imagine, and God wanted them.

Ah yes, you could be about to say, surely it was a case of finding a diamond in the rough – surely they were brilliant and wonderful underneath it all and God had done an *Antiques Roadshow* job, pulling out a gem from a load of old tat. Much as I'd like to go along with you there, I'm forced to disagree. Not only were they victims, but the Israelites were also a bit crap. Not long after they had been set free they started to whinge. They moaned so much that God decided to postpone their arrival in the promised land until they had learnt to trust and obey him. What was in fact a journey that should have taken a matter of months ended up lasting for forty years, simply because of their incessant whining.

But still God stayed with them. They were rightfully his and had been sinned against. That ignited a fiery passion within him that made him step in and intervene, particularly through faithful types like Moses. Over the years that followed he blessed, forgave, corrected and stuck by the people he had chosen over all the others. Why? Because he was committed to them, even when they were poor and lost. In time they wandered so far away from him that he sent his Son to bring not only them back, but also the rest of us.

The co-ordinates of Jesus's birth should come as no surprise; he was to be the most important man in the history of the world, but he was born a refugee. His words are still remembered today, yet he had no great political influence. He changed not only our lives, but also our deaths. He showed us exactly what God was like and he was born poor, oppressed and an outsider. Later, when he went about the business of setting up his team of workers that would change humanity for ever, he picked another bunch of intellectually challenged muppets. Do you see the pattern?

There's even more evidence on the bench when you start to look at some of the things that Jesus did during the final years of his life. As well as being poor and hanging round with some of the less brilliant people in society, Jesus chose some even more obvious ways to express the nature of God's heart, by showing the full intensity of his emotions.

The killer passage for checking out Jesus's passion is probably when he raises Lazarus from the dead. He knew the family – Lazarus' sister Mary was the woman who poured perfume on his feet and wiped them with her hair – and it was obviously no secret that he and Lazarus were friends. Mary and her sister Martha sent a message out to Jesus telling him, 'Lord, the one you love is sick', but for some reason Jesus took his time getting there. When he eventually did arrive, Lazarus had been in his tomb for four days. Mary was understandably a little upset about this, and when she first saw Jesus she fell at his feet and told him that if he had been there earlier her brother would still be alive.

> When Jesus saw her weeping, and the Jews who had come along with her also weeping, he was deeply moved in spirit and troubled. 'Where have you laid him?' he asked.
>
> 'Come and see, Lord,' they replied.
>
> Jesus wept.
>
> Then the Jews said, 'See how he loved him!'
>
> But some of them said, 'Could not he who opened the eyes of the blind man have kept this man from dying?'
>
> Jesus, once more deeply moved, came to the tomb. It was a cave with a stone laid across the entrance. 'Take away the stone,' he said.
>
> 'But, Lord,' said Martha, the sister of the dead man, 'by this time, there is a bad odour . . .'
>
> (John 11:33–9)

That line about there being a bad odour has most certainly been cleaned up along the way. The Greek word could be better translated as 'stink', which is not surprising considering that the corpse had been festering in the heat for four days. By that time decomposition would have been well under way and the odour would have been a lot worse than a polite, handkerchief-to-the-nose 'bad'.

> Then Jesus said, 'Did I not tell you that if you believed, you would see the glory of God?'
>
> So they took away the stone. Then Jesus looked up and said, 'Father, I thank you that you have heard me. I knew that you always hear me but I said this for the benefit of the people standing here that they might believe that you sent me.'
>
> When he had said this he called in a loud voice, 'Lazarus, come out!' The dead man came out, his hands and feet wrapped with strips of linen and a cloth around his face.
>
> Jesus said to them, 'Take off the grave clothes and let him go.'

It's easy to lose some of the emotion in this passage. Jesus's little aside to God about saying thank you for the sake of the crowd makes it seem as though he was a smooth cabaret act. The 'bad odour' takes away from the reality that many of the people would have spontaneously thrown up when the stone was rolled away. The fact that Jesus held back for a couple of days before he left for Lazarus' town could lead us to think that he was pretty unfussed about the whole thing.

All of these interpretations detract from the fact that this is one of the most intense scenes in Jesus's life. His friend had died. He had spent quite a bit of time with Lazarus and his two sisters, but needed Lazarus to be completely kaput in order for his miracle to have maximum impact. Even though he was aware that he had the power to bring him back to life, Jesus must have found it hard to prolong the pain of a family that he knew and loved. Perhaps that is why he did stay away, as to be around them and sense their agony would have made it too difficult to hold out for such a long time.

ANGRY AT INJUSTICE

So even before Jesus arrives on the scene we can be sure that emotions were running high. As soon as he does turn up and meets Mary who is deeply distressed, he too is 'deeply moved in spirit and troubled'. Approaching the tomb he weeps.

Now for ages when I read that bit of Scripture I thought, 'Oh, that's nice; dear old Jesus wept with Mary.' I thought the fact that the Jews commented, 'See how much he loves him,' meant that he was deeply sympathetic to her pain. I have a suspicion now though, that this isn't the reason for the weeping. The word that is translated here as 'deeply moved' comes from the Greek word which could also be translated 'groaned inside'. Another way that the phrase could have been translated which would also have been completely justified would have been 'Jesus was livid'. But our translators, perhaps keen to maintain an image of Jesus as gentle, have deliberately left it ambiguous. I suspect that the harder translation is more accurate.

Jesus was so angry with the situation that, when he saw the people who had no hope weeping, people who had failed to realise that life stood in the midst of them, his emotions came to the surface for all to see.

If you don't believe that Jesus gets angry, then look at the passage again in which he walks into the court of the Gentiles in the temple where they've got a bit of a tuck shop going (see Mark 11:12–19). Seeing that they were selling stuff for profit in a place where they should have been worshipping, he was so angry that he made a kind of whip and beat them up. Whatever way you put it, he was angry.

And Jesus was angry in this situation, just as he is furious today with injustice, pain and oppression. He wept over one man's death, much as he weeps today over the people yet to find him through their spiritual life. Sometimes we like to think that Jesus sits in heaven and wrings his hands, wincing and worrying about things but without actually feeling passionate enough to do anything. That's wrong, for whenever he sees injustice and the lost, whenever he comes across that which conflicts with his nature, he cannot be anything other than 'deeply moved'.

Approaching the tomb and telling the people to open it, there was obviously a certain amount of doubt as to the wisdom of his plan. While people were worried about a hygiene risk, Jesus asked them if they wanted to see the glory of God. He gave the choice over to them, in a sense making them take responsibility for what happened next. Imagine if they'd moved the stone away and Jesus had said, 'Good, lads, I'm off.' They would have been in serious trouble for desecrating something that was, in Jewish culture, a holy thing. You didn't open up a grave, not if you wanted to carry on living.

They took the risk. Once the tomb was open, Jesus started praying. We're not sure how long it took, but you can be sure that with every passing moment, with every furtive glance back and forth between the hole and Jesus the tension would have increased. The tension wouldn't have been over once Jesus had shouted to Lazarus to come out either, as seeing a four-day-old corpse come shuffling out of a graveyard was hardly an everyday sight. I'm sure there would have been screams and tears of both delight and fear. Finally he told the people to take off Lazarus' grave clothes. Far from being a dry and clinical show of God's power, the raising of Lazarus was about as emotionally charged as you could possibly imagine.

Only Jesus can speak to the physically dead and bring them back to life. Only Jesus can speak to the spiritually dead and bring them back to life. He gets angry when he sees injustice and weeps when he sees the lost.

The old saying, 'If a job's worth doing it's worth doing yourself', probably means nothing to God. Sure he is infinitely more capable than any of us, but life for God is not just about efficiency: it's about relationship. Whenever God sees something to be done he looks around for his people to get stuck in. When he freed the Israelites he first called Moses. When he set up the Church, he first called the disciples. When he raised Lazarus from the dead he first got the mourners to pull back the stone. When Lazarus was out in the open Jesus told the people to remove his grave clothes, giving him a fresh start.

Don't get me wrong though: I'm not saying that we could accomplish all this on our own. Have you tried raising the dead recently? It's not the easiest of jobs to tackle. God created us so that he could share his love with us. We're still signed up for the partnership, and we're still in line for some jobs.

Just as he has done throughout history, God even today wants us to get closer to him in order to take his love out. He wants us to roll away the stones that separate others from him, whether that means releasing them from poverty or oppression or bringing light into their spiritual darkness. He wants us to take off the grave clothes, to disciple and rebuild the lives decomposed by the effects of long-term sin.

Jesus told us plain and simple that he only did

what he saw the Father do. He also told us to go – to make disciples, to baptise, to teach and to love – in the same way that he did. We just cannot get out of the fact that God's heart beats wildly for his people, and that he is desperate to heal – using our hands.

This isn't the time to wait: this is the time to soak up some of the passion of our almighty God and see where we end up.

7

United We Stand

GLORY, GLORY...

Long before I was given my first trousers, I was
given my first football pyjamas. And my first
football comb. And my first football zip-up raincoat.
In fact, as far as I was concerned, while there was
still football merchandise being sold long trousers
could go hang. I had so much football stuff that for
over a year I had a recurring dream that my bedroom floor would give in under the weight of it all,
sending me hurtling down towards the ground only
to have my fall broken by the mid-field section of
the 1967 Brighton and Hove Albion team. I don't
know why it was Brighton and Hove Albion in the
dream, since for as long as I can remember I
have had eyes for one team and one team only:
Manchester United. As a child I was obsessed with
them, and everything I owned was red and white

101

with their logo taking pride of place. By the time my knees were no longer seeing regular sunlight and my parents had got me into long trousers I had collected enough Man U merchandise to write to *The Guinness Book of Records* and ask if I was the biggest football fan in the world. I wasn't. Depressed by their cold-hearted reply I decided to get myself a life and reduce my level of support from visibly fanatical to quietly obsessive.

I'm proud to say that Man U and I are still going strong, and that like any true supporter I've never actually seen them play at Old Trafford. Being a Man U fan these days isn't easy though, especially with the people who've just climbed aboard since they've been winning everything. I was there when things were tough, when we won nothing, when the rain beat down hard upon the cold streets . . .

Sorry about that, it's just that those dark days still make me feel slightly emotional. Anyway, back to business. You see, the thing about supporting them is that in all the years that have passed I've never been so impressed as I was in the 1998–9 season. No other time can compare to the rollercoaster ride that took place from August to May, and it wasn't just the fact of winning the treble – a feat never before achieved in the history of English football – but it was the way we won that left me speechless. It is no exaggeration to say that United are now the English national team.

But don't worry, I'm not writing this just to gloat – although that is a very pleasant by-product – I believe that there are some fundamental lessons that we Christians can learn from Manchester United's glory season.

BE PREPARED

Without doubt David Beckham is one of the best players in the world. In fact, when it comes to free kicks and corners, he's probably the best dead-ball specialist there has ever been. (In case you're wondering this means he's good at kicking the ball from a fixed position, not that he's good when there's no air left inside it, although I wouldn't put it past him.) The Adidas TV advert that accompanied the 1998 World Cup showed him curling a ball round a huge stone structure and into a less than huge gap. Obviously the lad's got talent, but if you think he got where he is today simply because of his gifting, you would be wrong.

I've got an interview with Beckham on video in which he's asked what the secret is of his goal scoring abilities. 'I practised, that's what I done,' he replies. 'When I was a kid I used to kick a ball against the wall for hours. I'd kick it with my right foot, and then I'd kick it with my left foot. I'd kick it with my dad and I'd kick it on my own. I practised, that's all I done.'

He's not alone, as his best mate Gary Neville, the United and England defender, will admit. Neville's not the most naturally talented footballer in the world, and as a schoolboy he was the one watching from the side while his brother played for England. United boss Alex Ferguson has said that what impressed him about Gary Neville was his dedication. When the training session is over and all the others are climbing into their Italian suits, little Gary will be on his own going back out onto the pitch to practise some more. His skill and talent have been developed by sheer hard work, making him now one of the best defenders in England.

So what's my point? Well, as Christians we are often exceptionally talented at waiting for God to wave his magic wand and make our lives wonderful. We hang around with folded arms waiting for a chance to do something in public – whether it's playing in a band, preaching or leading a project – unwilling to put any serious hard graft in. Sometimes we'll sit back and declare to God that it's up to him to land us a top job in a prestigious company without even considering that we might have to play a part in the delivery.

This is partly because we have made things too spiritual and partly because we're lazy. The spiritual thing is a result of our believing that if we just pray hard enough then God will sort everything out. Unfortunately that's not the way it works. Think about Jesus – wouldn't it have been easier for God to get involved with some hefty spiritual warfare up there in the spiritual realm than send his own Son down to spend over three decades working hard as a human? No, God knows the value of hard work and we need to do a little revision.

Because we rule out the option of taking some of the responsibility for things ourselves, we seem to spend a fair amount of time staring at closed or only slightly open doors. Too many Christians are lazy with their gifts and then wonder why God doesn't use them more. When David (king, that is) was anointed by Samuel to be king over Israel you might have expected him to hang around the palace until the coronation, soaking up the vibes and getting accustomed to a life of luxury. After all, being king was an important position, and surely it would have made sense to get acquainted with things. Instead young King David went back to being a shepherd and worked hard at being the best shepherd that he could. While he was busy doing that, God made sure that nothing was wasted, and with the sheep he learned many skills which were to come in useful later on. He learned the lessons of battle as he fought with the lions and bears which tried to attack his sheep. They were particularly useful when it came to sorting out fat-boy Goliath, but were also helpful when he took on the role of commander of his army later on. Caring for his flock taught him how to care for his people, pastoring and leading them through treacherous circumstances. He also wrote his best worship song (Psalm 23) out on the hills as the little bleaters were grazing. Like Moses – who received his preparation for the task of leading Israel out of slavery by spending forty years in the desert – David's teaching ground was unglamorous, private and dangerous.

Even the Lord Jesus had thirty years of preparation for three years of ministry. If David Beckham and Gary Neville were willing to prepare themselves so thoroughly in order to be the best footballers they could be, why aren't we training ourselves and preparing for the highest calling we could have: to serve the living God. If your passion is to lead worship, don't wait until you are asked to play at Soul Survivor or Spring Harvest; prepare now, prac- tise on your musical instrument now, wait on the Lord now. If you think your calling is to be an evangelist, learn all you can about communication skills now, read all the evangelistic books you can now. Whatever your dream, kick the ball against the wall now, and then when the opportunity comes you will be ready.

BE FAMILY

Footballers aren't known for being the most self-sacrificing and humble of people. They earn vast sums of money and work in an industry that constantly compares them against each other. When it comes to most teams, it doesn't take much to see the cracks and work out where the divisions and disharmony lie. One of the unusual and extraordinary things about Manchester United is the way the team seem to get on so well. When Dwight Yorke arrived at the beginning of the season the press was having a field day speculating about whether he would replace their other main striker Andy Cole. For weeks the contest was talked up and the two players were portrayed as rivals for the same position. What happened behind the scenes was that they quickly became best friends off the pitch and established an inspiring rapport on it as a result. After a couple of months most people agreed that Andy Cole had become a better player since Dwight Yorke arrived.

When Beckham was sent off in that fateful World Cup game against Argentina he became one of the most hated men in England. There were death threats, burning effigies, rumours that the only way he could ever survive in the game would be to move to an Italian club for a couple of years. Back home where he belonged though, his manager and team-mates rallied round in his time of need and supported him in many ways. He stayed, worked through it, and within months had fought his way back to the top and regained the respect he had lost. Beckham has even been quoted as saying that as a result of all the support he received he wants to play for Manchester United for the rest of his career.

If there can be such a sense of team spirit in a football club, how much more should that be evident in the Church of Jesus Christ? We are commanded by our Lord to love one another as he has loved us. Try reading that line again . . . love each other as he loved us. Considering that Jesus's love took him all the way to the cross, I would say that loving each other in the same manner is a pretty radical thing. One of the images of the Church in the Bible is that of family. Instead, all too often there is backbiting, competitiveness and gossip. We sometimes seem to forget that we are all playing on the same side, and get weighed down with concepts of right and wrong. You don't even have to go so far as to look at the wars that have been fought in the name of Christianity, as you talk to many churchgoers, sadly most local churches will be defined more by the things that people are unhappy with rather than the things that they like.

We are often uncomfortable at church. We tell other people what we think they want to hear –

spiritual whitewash that has about as much to do with the reality of how we are actually feeling as drinking a sports drink makes you fit. Instead of being honest we tell people that everything is just fine, that 'me and the Lord are doing well'. What we really want to say is, 'I don't like church and I don't even know if God exists any more.' We've all been there but few of us have actually admitted it at the time. But if we cannot be honest, how then can we be close? If we cannot be real, how can we be family? Do you think that Beckham would have been so touched by the reception that his team-mates gave him if it had gone along the lines of 'Never mind old chap, so what if you are hated by every football supporter in England? Isn't the pitch looking lovely today?'

No, real families are made up of real people, ones that call difficulties exactly what they are, and don't skirt round them with 'Oh yes, but isn't the Lord good'. Jesus never shied away from expressing his stronger emotions: he wept at Lazarus' tomb, was in torment in the garden of Gethsemane, got livid in the temple (twice) and preached with all the passion of someone who knows he is right. If we are going to follow him, church should be a place where we are free to express exactly how we feel, safe in the knowledge that it will provide love and support without strings or condemnation.

PLAY FOR THE TEAM

One of the players I most admired at United during the 1998/9 season was the Norwegian international Ole Gunner Solskjaer. He started out most matches as a substitute, but in the relatively short time that he spent on the pitch, he managed to notch up for himself more goals than the scorers at fourteen out of the twenty-one other clubs in the premiership. When it came to the F.A. Cup final, Solskjaer found himself in the starting line-up in his favourite forward position. After five minutes of the game the United skipper Roy Keane went off injured and Teddy Sheringham was brought on to replace him. Solskjaer had to switch positions to the right wing where, playing out of position, he frankly did not excel. A reason to be unhappy, you may think, but that's not true. As one match commentator said at the time, Solskjaer had 'sacrificed himself for the sake of the team'. He played where he was least comfortable and least likely to shine simply because it was exactly what the team needed at that moment.

Many Christians could learn a valuable lesson from Solskjaer. Instead of always wanting to be the one scoring the spiritual goals, we need to ask ourselves if we are willing to sometimes serve in an area which is not our favourite. For the sake of the team, for the sake of the Kingdom, are we prepared to do something that goes unnoticed, something that could easily be ignored, let alone forgotten? Are you a team player or are you a lone ranger Christian, striding on ahead of the rest, pursuing your own spiritual ambitions while the rest of the team are wondering where you've got to? In the Kingdom there is only one hero, Jesus, and if we are ever going to achieve our goal of making disciples of all nations we have to learn to play as a team under his captaincy.

NEVER GIVE UP

There is so much teaching in the Bible about persistence, and of all their many attributes, the one for which Manchester United will be remembered the most is that they refused to give up. In the F.A. Cup quarter-final against Liverpool, United were one–nil down with two minutes to go. When the final whistle blew after two minutes of injury time they had won two–one. In the Champions' League semi-final against Juventus they were two–nil down going into the second half. They won three–two. Most famously of all, they were losing to Bayern Munich in that great final with ninety minutes gone. Those two goals, first by Sheringham and then by Solskjaer with virtually the last kick of the match, are moments no United fan will ever forget. Sir Alex Ferguson said after the match, 'These players just don't know how to give in.' You could say there was an element of luck in the way they scored last-minute goals so many times, but they made their own luck by perseverance and persistence.

Winston Churchill was once asked what he thought the secret of leadership was. His reply was, 'Never give in, never give in, never give in.' Surely as the children of the Almighty who know we are on the winning side, we ought to never grow weary but persist in doing good. That means refusing to ditch the faith whenever we get knocked back. It means carrying on with God despite the fact that church may be frustrating or our leaders might be sad. Sticking with Jesus in the face of ridicule and pressure is something we will all have to do if we want to grow up in our relationship with God. Like any marriage, sacking the whole thing at the slightest disagreement is a foolish waste, and God has so much in store for us that to drop him whenever we feel like it is a choice I hope you and I never make. Steve Chalke, a TV presenter and the director of Oasis Trust, was once asked what he considered to be his greatest strength. His reply surprised me. He said, 'I'm a plodder. I keep going. Whether it's a good day or a bad day, I put my head down and keep going.'

Let us be ready for all that God has for us. Let us encourage and support one another. Let us serve one another and put each other first. And then let us play the match with all we have until we hear the final whistle. That's what Man United do – just think how much more we could achieve if we set our minds to it.

8

The Next Step

FEELING USELESS

Ever get that feeling that you're on your own? You know how it goes – a holiday draws to a close and you find yourself back at home, dealing with a come-down that makes everything seem grey and pointless. I get it a lot – coming back from trips abroad or festivals where I've seen the most amazing things happen and have felt 100 per cent on fire for God. Often, the journey back will be my time to think about things and get excited about what I might be in line for seeing God do next. Something happens on the way through the front door though, as usually by the time I've picked up the post and put my bags down, I've forgotten everything that had me feeling so great just moments before. I feel dull and hopeless, and in desperate need of some Chinese therapy. Usually a bag full of beef in black bean sauce with a double helping of banana fritters helps to pull me through the next few hours, but I'm still a mere shadow of my former turbo-charged self.

Knowing that it's going to hit me doesn't help much either, as everything I've tried in an effort to avoid the homecoming blues has more or less failed to keep me from feeling down. I've tried having friends over, walking through the door backwards and not returning home at all. All that these left me with was a sense of extreme embarrassment that I left the flat in such a state before the trip, a severe bruise on the back of my head and a warning from the chairwoman of my local neighbourhood watch scheme that if I spent one more night sleeping in my car she would be forced to have me arrested on suspicion of being an illegal immigrant.

In short, when I'm at the end of a trip, I'm useless. I might have been preaching as well as I possibly can, maybe even using some of my own material instead of stealing it from other people, but as soon as the environment changes I feel like I'm about as wise as a cardboard monkey.

I was whining about this to a friend of mine recently when he told me to shut up and use my brain. I tried, but nothing happened. He told me to think about the disciples, about how they felt at the end of their trip with Jesus. Again, no result. Eventually, after a lot of work, it became clear. If ever there was a trip to have a come-down from, it was immediately after the death of Jesus. Imagine how close they must have grown – living together for three years, seeing things that no one else had ever seen before. In time they realised that they were hanging around with the Messiah, the man who had been prophesied about and who every fellow Jew was waiting for. To talk about their time together in terms of a buzz doesn't do it justice, but it does explain that they had every reason to feel low afterwards.

Guess what? There's a *but* coming. You see, Jesus knew this – being fully man he knew how they would feel – and so he put them through an intense course during their final days together, preparing them for the future. Jesus's life was too important to be confined to the photo album; it had to carry on, and Jesus made sure that the people he had chosen to train were well equipped to carry things on after he had gone. More importantly, though, Jesus knew that in speaking to the disciples, he was speaking to all Christians that would sign up with him in the years to come. Jesus was speaking to us, telling us how to carry on, how to live our lives in a way that would keep us going forward instead of slouching in a corner complaining about how things aren't so much fun when Jesus isn't around to give a spectacular display of spiritual fireworks.

First of all he left us with a great commandment. Matthew 22:37–40 is our own personal mission statement, pre-packed and sealed for guaranteed satisfaction any place, any time. 'What is the greatest commandment?' asked one of the religious big boys.

> Jesus replied: ' "Love the Lord your God with all your heart and with all your soul and with all your mind." This is the first and greatest commandment. And the second is like it: "Love your neighbour as yourself." All the Law and the Prophets hang on these two commandments.'

This summary that Jesus left us with really couldn't put things any clearer. Into our life-stew should go just two basic ingredients: a full-on love for God and a sacrificial love for those around us.

He also left us with cooking instructions. Later on in the book of Matthew we find Jesus's final words, generally referred to as the Great Commission.

> Then Jesus came to them and said, 'All authority in heaven and on earth has been given to me. Therefore go and make disciples of all nations, baptising them in the name of the Father and of the Son and of the Holy Spirit, and teaching them to obey everything I have commanded you. And surely I am with you always, to the very end of the age.' (Matthew 28:18–20)

So there we have it – the ingredients and the method. The Great Commandment tells us how we are to live and the Great Commission tells us why we've been left on planet earth. Jesus made it so clear, breaking it down into such bite-sized portions that even the most awkward among us can be clear about what we Christians should be doing.

POWER TO LIVE

Obviously now that I've reached the age of forty-one I've started to entertain the possibility that at some point in the future I might not be on the cutting-edge of contemporary fashion. It's understandable, I suppose, but still, after so long spent being so cool, it does feel funny to think about one day sitting back and letting new things take over. I decided to get in some practice on this recently. Midway through one summer I started to notice that not everyone was following my fashion lead by wearing nylon smocks covered with African art. It seemed that someone was convincing them to opt for a different trend, namely bracelets. Now, I've never really been into jewellery, but I had to admit that this particular fashion had gone big time.

These fabric bracelets were everywhere – assuming you were at a Christian festival, that is – and on them were embroidered the letters WWJD. Standing for What Would Jesus Do?, some clever American businessperson with a flair for marketing had developed a whole lifestyle around a simple product.

The idea with them was that the wearer would have a constant reminder to think about what Jesus would do at any given time. This all kind of ties in with the Great Stew mentioned above, especially as loving God and your neighbours as well as making disciples are things that can apply to any situation we find ourselves in.

I don't think that it was because I was jealous or feeling left out, but as I thought about them, something didn't quite fit. Let me explain. In case you've picked up and have only started reading the book at this late stage, I am a Manchester United supporter. It stands to reason, therefore, that one of my main heroes is Mr Beckham. He's an inspirational player, and definitely a good on-the-pitch role-model for any fan (assuming that we have forgiven him for responding to a provoked attack from Simeone in the World Cup game against Argentina in 1998). If I played football – and I don't – I would definitely consider wearing a WWBD? bracelet. Lining up for a free kick I would glance down and ask myself, what would Beckham do? The answer would come back in the form of one of those *Match of the Day* highlights, with our David curling the ball around the wall, past the scrambling goalie and into the top right-hand corner of the net. Simple. Or maybe we're in the park, right in the middle of some free-flowing play. Spoddy Harris has made a darting run down the left wing and I'm faced with a couple of mid-field thugs bearing down on me with the intention of doing some serious bodily harm to my fragile frame. What would Beckham do? He'd take the ball to them, move it over to one side and deliver a perfectly placed pass onto the Spodster, leaving him with an open goal and no pressure from the thugs. Again, beautifully simple. But, back to reality, what would I do? In the case of a free kick I'd probably mistime my approach, drive my foot into the ground, spraining my ankle and leaving the ball untouched. When it comes to thugs the chances are that I'd leave the ball where it was, forget about Spoddy Harris and make a run for the safety of the touchline. It's all very well *knowing* what he would do, the trick is being *able* to carry it off.

David Beckham can do a whole load of things that I can't do: he can play football, pull a Spice Girl and wear his clothes with style and panache. Even though some have said that I do remind them of him, having a WWBD? thing on my arm would be worse than useless, it would actually be incredibly frustrating. And so we come back to the Bible. Just to have the Great Commandment and the Great Commission is not enough. To have a constant reminder of what we ought to be doing is helpful, it certainly gives us something to aim at, but if we have trouble trying to copy Becks, how the heck can we hope to pull off a decent imitation of the Son of God?

Thankfully, Jesus saw this problem before it

happened, and prepared for us the ultimate antidote to the frustration that comes from not being able to reach our goals. He gave us power. We're not just talking about the power to blag it or the power to fool others, but the raw power to do what he did, and then some.

The book of Acts kicks off with a description of the time Jesus spent with his disciples after he had risen from the dead. At one meal time he told them not to leave Jerusalem until they had received the gift that had been promised. When they pressed him for some more info on this, asking whether it meant the end of time, he replied:

> He said to them: 'It is not for you to know the times or dates the Father has set by his own authority. But you will receive power when the Holy Spirit comes on you; and you will be my witnesses in Jerusalem, and in all Judea and Samaria, and to the ends of the earth.' (Acts 1:7–8)

When Jesus gave the Great Commission he didn't leave us powerless or unable to follow through. Instead he packaged it up as part of the ultimate Two-for-One deal: If you sign up for the vision, you get the power. But, unlike most Two-for-One deals, this is a darn sight more useful than 1.5 litres of extra non-biological colour-fast washing liquid. This power is dynamite, and with it, the early Church changed the shape of things to come. If you don't believe me all you have to do is read through the book of Acts and check out for yourself the intense relationship that existed between the way they relied on the power that Jesus had given them through the Holy Spirit and the mind-blowing rate of growth that the Church experienced.

They were effective in ways that we as a Church today long to be effective – they reached all sectors of society, exploded with a force never before seen and took beatings and persecution without dropping their belief that Jesus was their ultimate Saviour. In short, the early Church were riding high on a cocktail of obedience and power. Guess what, it's still on the menu.

Some of us need to be reminded of the fact that Jesus gave us the power to carry out the 'To Do' list that he left us with. Some of us need to be reminded that Jesus's offer still stands, and that all we have to do is step up and take it. Of course, doing this means that we have to acknowledge the fact that we *can't* do things in our own strength. It means humbling ourselves and admitting that without God's help, we are unable to achieve all that is expected of us. No matter how intelligent, charming, good looking or threatening we are, winning the lost for God is totally dependent on our using God's power. What Acts shows us is a practical outworking of the power of

God in run-of-the-mill daily situations; it was there to give them boldness when they preached, to give them a love for one another as well as the poor so that they could carry out the works of the Kingdom. But it also meant that they could perform signs and wonders that accompanied their preaching, it meant that they had the power to set people free.

I am convinced that God wants to release that power on us again so that our words and actions would have that extra bite that transforms them into building blocks for the Kingdom of God. I'm not saying that God ever withdrew his gifts, I'm just convinced that we have spent far too long ignoring the fact that Jesus gave us a helping hand. Just like me when I get back from a trip and feel miserable, we've been doing things in our own strength, forgetting that Jesus offers us the power to see things through, the power to rise above our own strength and onto another level.

There's another treat at the bottom of our stocking though: Jesus didn't just give us the power to follow the rules, he also gave us the power to change and become more like him. In John 15 we get a wonderful picture of Jesus as the vine with us as the branches. 'If you remain in me and my words remain in you,' Jesus tells us, 'you will bear fruit.' That means that we don't just have the opportunity to produce more signs of being like Christ, but that we actually can *become* more like Christ, as the fruit is the character of Jesus in our lives.

I don't know about you, but I certainly could do with a helping dose of change. I need to be more like the kind of Mike Pilavachi that God had in mind when he made me and less of the kind of Mike Pilavachi that has since been moulded by the world around me. I've tried changing in my own strength; I've tried concentrating, dieting and shouting my way towards perfection, but nothing has worked. I need the power of Jesus to complete the job – and just in the same way that I need him for salvation, I also need him for the power to change.

Sitting in my car outside my flat, a delicate hum coming from my bag stuffed full of unclean pants and industrially toxic socks, I have sometimes wondered whether it would be possible to pull myself out of the grouchy mood I'm in and put a brave face on it. Possibly, but unlikely. The trouble is that emotions are strong things, and the chances of me being able to override them are a little on the slim side.

GOD'S AUTHORITY

The thing about Jesus is that he not only talked about power, he talked about authority. He didn't just give us the ability to follow his lead, he also had the authority that sent him straight to the head of the queue. His Father had given him authority to act with the full weight of heaven behind him, and that weight meant that he could go right to the heart of things. Think of it as if you were an amazing dancer, able to outgroove any person in any club. The trouble comes when you try to get in – the bouncers don't like you and stop you from entering the clubs. Imagine having a pass that allowed you to swan past even the most grumpy of doormen. You can get in and shake your booty wherever you want and everything's lovely. The power is the moves and the authority is the pass.

For an example of this just think about the story of Jesus healing the paralytic man (Mark 2:1–12). Midway through a seminar in someone's house, a hole appears in the roof and down comes a guy on a mat. His mates were lowering him down, and amidst the chaos and confusion, Jesus performed one of his most significant miracles. He looked at him and said, 'Your sins are forgiven.' This was like going from the frying pan into the fire, and the place erupted. The top-dog religious people simply couldn't understand what made Jesus think that he had the authority to forgive someone's sin. More or less Jesus replied that he forgave sins by the same authority that he told people to walk; in other words, his was a direct power-feed from heaven, and he had the ability to act as God, forgiving sins and restoring life.

There was another incident with a high-ranking Roman soldier (Matthew 8:5–13). His servant was ill and he needed Jesus's help. Unusually, though, he didn't ask Jesus to come and visit the boy. This centurion recognised something in Jesus that others missed; he recognised that Jesus was far and away more in control of the situation than many suspected. People knew he could perform miracles, but remote miracles? Ones where he was a long way off and unable to lay hands on the patient?

The centurion gave away his thoughts by opening up his conversation with Jesus with a chat about authority. He told Jesus that he didn't need to visit, but just to say the word and his servant would be healed. The soldier told Jesus that he understood the nature of authority, especially as he was the kind of guy who was used to giving orders and seeing them carried out. His faith impressed Jesus, so much so that he commented how he had not seen faith as strong in the whole of Israel. He did as he was asked and healed the lad. The centurion understood that it wasn't only about power, but that the ability to harness the influence of heaven made all the difference.

This relates to us in the Church today. We've got kind of used to the idea of power being around – we've seen people healed and lives changed – but we've forgotten that we do actually have authority over all things. Now authority might not be the coolest of words to use – after all, these days we're into each person being right and no one being wrong – but it's true; when it comes to the crunch, God has allowed us to hitch a ride on the back of his power and claim some of it for ourselves.

Read how Jesus sent the disciples out to do his work:

> When Jesus had called the Twelve together, he gave them power and authority to drive out all demons and to cure diseases, and he sent them out to preach the kingdom of God and to heal the sick. (Luke 9:1–2)

That was the twelve. Later he does it with a group of seventy-two. Throughout the book of Acts we can see how even more of the first followers respond to this sending out from Jesus. They were persecuted and they were weak. They had martyrs and they went without any of the legal protection that we have today, but they had *real* power and *real* authority because it came from heaven above.

Not long ago I spent ten days in California speaking at a festival. Three of us went out there to do what we thought was a 'normal' trip, giving out to other people, praying and all that stuff. I tell you, we returned in a complete state. We were exhausted but on the biggest spiritual high we had ever been on. We had stayed with a family who were 100 per cent committed to praying for people and hearing from God 100 per cent of the time. It didn't matter where we were – having a meal, getting ready to go out or driving in the car – they were always on the look out for actively getting Jesus involved in the situation. Not only did we get some physical healing, but we also had some amazingly profound things told us that just had to be from God. It was astounding how accurate they were, and coming back, I almost got tempted to feel a bit down and to start to miss it. Somehow my mood didn't go any further, and I started thinking about what Jesus had done for us. The only difference between the Californian family and me was that they knew that they had the power and authority that came direct from heaven. Knowing that, their lives were a rollercoaster of faith in action.

God's power and authority are continually on offer to us. There is no need for us to beg for them; they've already been given. All that remains is for us to reach out and take them. Finally, let's not get sold the lie of thinking that power and authority are optional extras, put up on offer just to make the ride a little smoother, should we need them. Let's not get it into our heads that we're too cool or too cynical to grab hold of Jesus-style acts of power and authority. This is important, so much so it could be what makes the difference between sitting grumpily on the sidelines, complaining that God never uses us and being in the thick of it, enjoying the full extent of the essence of God. If we are to reach the lost we need to preach the gospel with wise and persuasive words and all the tools and gifts that he has given us. But more than that, we need to obey the Great Commandment – loving the Lord with all that we have as well as loving our neighbour as we love ourselves – as when the world sees a Church that's in love with its God and loving towards themselves it will be attracted to that God. We also need to know that the Great Commission is for us. Right here. Right now.